Golf - More than just a swing!
Linking Mind, Body, Technique & Instinct

By

Nicky Lawrenson

Copyright © 2020 Nicky Lawrenson

All rights reserved.

This ebook is licensed for your personal enjoyment only. This ebook may not be re-sold or given away to other people. If you would like to share this ebook with another person, please purchase an additional copy for each person you share it with. If you're reading this book and did not purchase it, or it was not purchased for your use only, then you should purchase your own copy. Thank you for respecting the hard work of this author.

Ebook formatting by ebooklaunch.com

For my mum & dad, Phil & Wendy. Thank you for everything.

Table of Contents

Introduction 1

Getting The Most From Your Coaching & Practice Sessions 5

The Key To Becoming Your Own Best Coach 16

The Technology Of Coaching 28

Eliminating The Destructive 36

Quick Fix Versus Long Term Development 42

One Size Fits All – Or Does It?! 46

The Power Sources 50

The Short Stuff 69

The Mid Round Slump 79

Why Isn't This Positive Thinking Working?! 87

The Emotional Scale 99

Believing Is Seeing 122

The Golfing Mind – Breaking The Pattern 133

Imagery 141

The Fear Factor! 150

East Meets West – Breathing, Physiology & Mr Miyagi! 164

The Power Of Focus 174

The Mind-Body Connection, What The Science Says 183

Perception – The Filters Of Success 194

The Pitfalls Of A Perfectionist 199

Trust 209

Guiding The Young Golfer 215

Epilogue 221

End Notes 224

INTRODUCTION

My most important aim in writing this book is to help provide a simplified understanding of the golf swing and help you gain as much success and enjoyment from your game as possible. There is a great deal of information readily available within the golfing world and it can become a confusing minefield and a little overwhelming at times. You may have felt the frustration of trying a tip you have read, and finding it seems to work for a few holes or at best, a few days, and then all of a sudden things slip back how they were! The frustrating cycle then begins all over again. You feel lost in a void of what to do with your swing next. This is not to disregard or disrespect the quality of the information or its benefits. I do, however, believe there are a few key factors involved with this scenario that when understood and implemented can help prevent the frustrations and never ending search for the 'Magic Answer! ' So as much as this book is not intended to be a 'how to' instructional breakdown of the golf swing, there are some fantastic sources of information currently available online or in print that provide just that, it is designed to assist in steering you along a more consistent and simplified path, through an understanding aimed at preventing that continual search.

Its aim is to bring together a few simple understandings which, in my coaching experience, have enabled golfers to reduce their frustrations, clear a little confusion and enjoy their progress in the great game. I believe golf holds great parallels to how we live our lives both professionally and personally and provides a fantastic learning curve that enables us to enhance our well-being and performance both on and off the golf course.

In experimenting through the vast depths of information, many unnecessary frustrations can arise through trial and error of the unknown. You may try many different swing thoughts or concepts and ultimately feel you are declining as it becomes difficult to gain any form of consistency through constant change, you can then potentially feel back to square one. The information may be fantastic in its own right but is not necessarily applicable to you and your own individual golf swing. Every golfer is very individual and each person has their own individual wants, needs and aspirations and this must always be taken into full consideration when looking to develop and achieve goals. Golfers vary considerably, in many ways, such as physiology, mindset, age, ability, lifestyles and end goals. For these reasons I strongly believe that moulding around these differences to suit the individual in the best way possible can provide the most successful results rather than trying to fit each individual into one set model.

It is becoming ever more widely embraced within modern day coaching that the golfing mind can often become the missing link to success or under performance on the golf course. Mental and emotional mastery are hugely significant to not only performance on the golf course but within many areas of life itself. By gaining the self awareness to guide thoughts, emotions and ultimately beliefs into the path of what we want to achieve is hugely empowering and can determine success in both sport and life. Change begins when any limiting patterns of habit are broken and replaced with more positive, consistent and desire-focussed alternatives. The world of mental and emotional mastery covers philosophies from both the Eastern and Western cultures and the latest findings in neuroscience are continually affirming the scientific evidence about the mind-body connection. To ignore this connection with regards to our performance, I believe is leaving out a huge piece to the puzzle. My passion to delve into these latest findings, combined with the learning curve developed from my competitive years as a golfer and experience as a golf coach has led me to follow the path of unearthing the unlimited potential of the human mind both on and off the golf course. What I have learned is interwoven throughout this book with other key concepts that I feel enable golfers of all abilities to reach their full potential.

The chapters within the book address various aspects of the game including not only basic technical concepts but also looking at the importance of the mind and body as a whole. As the saying goes, 'The most highly tuned sports car cannot perform at its best if the fuel gauge is on empty or there is a monkey behind the wheel!' The emphasis in this book is to create an easy to understand and self empowering guide which enables you to develop a better understanding of your game with confidence and self sufficiency. It encourages you to master the art of becoming your own best coach.

Each chapter is designed in such a way that they may be picked up and read individually at leisure. The first half of the book has a little more emphasis on the technical elements to the game discussing amongst other aspects, if there really is a 'magic answer' and is a quick fix really the best option? The second half is devoted to achieving success from the inside out and it aims to offer an insight and guidance into how the mind-body connection provides such an important infrastructure to our performance. Collectively they endeavour to highlight the pillars that support the platform towards peak performance, well-being and enjoyment in the game of golf that so many of us love.

I truly hope that you enjoy this book and that it is beneficial. My ultimate goal as a coach is to enable each golfer to become as self sufficient as possible and ultimately become their own coach, which in turn leads to greater empowerment, satisfaction, enjoyment and most importantly, becomes more sustainable over time.

GETTING THE MOST FROM YOUR COACHING & PRACTICE SESSIONS

'Give a man a fish and you feed him one day, teach a man to fish and you will feed him for a lifetime'
- Maimonides

How can we, at times, feel as though we are putting so much effort into our games yet feel as though we are gaining little in return?! We've put hours in on the range, read every book and article, enjoyed success in our lessons only for it to be snatched cruelly away from us just days later!

The elusive magic move!

Our mindset, emotions and belief systems must be brought into the equation when discussing long term progress and improvement, however some of the frustrations involved with improving our game ride on the back of an unending and sometimes overwhelming search for the latest 'Magic Answer'. There is a huge resource and some fantastic information readily accessible at our fingertips whether via a magazine article, online video or instruction book and when used to our advantage, can provide great steps forward to improving our game. The flip side however, is that it can also create a never ending frustrating loop of 'find it, lose it, find it, lose it' within our games as we continue to experiment and search for the one piece of magic that will cure all. Continued experimentation, combined with an underlying uncertainty about the correct concept of our own golf swings, can make progress feel like an uphill battle.

So how can we achieve a more consistent flow of progress and get the most from our games, coaching and practice sessions? Let's simplify things. Having a good understanding of *your* swing in its *simplest* form is extremely helpful and is key to preventing that continual search. Often, when you locate the *primary* factor within your swing that may need a little attention, it tends to have a positive chain reaction and knock on effect on any sequences that follow. Understanding this and then simplifying the focal point can help the process greatly; avoid confusing yourself with an excessive overload of thoughts. There is often the worry that once one aspect of the swing has been developed or improved, focus should then shift to perfecting all other elements, i.e. backswing, downswing, impact and follow through. This isn't to say everything else will effortlessly fall into place, although at times that can happen too! But at least understanding the concept can help reduce the worry of trying to perfect every element in the golf swing or breaking the golf swing down into too many different technical components.

The importance of set up fundamentals and the chain reaction

The basic fundamentals of the set up (i.e. alignment, grip, posture, ball position and stance) play a pivotal role to a golfer's success and greatly enhance the opportunity for consistency. Underestimating the importance of the set up could prove a major stumbling block to any level of golfer. There can be the misperception that the set up and basic fundamentals are really only applicable to the beginner and once learnt can be put to one side, and not thought about again in the future. World-class players will ensure they work on the basic fundamentals if and where necessary. The body can only establish certain movements and positions that the original starting position allows. Therefore, if the set up is out of position in some way, there often has to be some form of compensatory move within the swing to recover from it. Solid fundamentals within the set up can make a significantly positive impact. If the fundamentals and foundations of the set up are incorrect in some way, this will have an impact on what the body is able to do from that point onwards. Generally, the better the set up, the better the take away; the better the takeaway the better the backswing and so the chain reaction continues. Of course **impact** is the critical area and we cannot guarantee that a perfect set up and backswing position will deliver a perfect impact position and certainly there are what would be classed as slightly more unorthodox ways to reach an ideal impact position, however, solid foundations will certainly help it happen more often and with greater ease. Every action in the swing has an equal and opposite reaction, the fewer reactions and compensations we have to make pre and post impact the easier the game becomes.

Creating a disciplined routine within the set up creates a stable platform and starting point for the golf swing. Just as unstable foundations of a house provide shaky ground for the remainder of the structure, poor fundamentals often mean the golf swing is playing catch up, and subsequent compensations will need to follow creating a breeding ground for inconsistency. The best players in the world realise the importance of the basics within golf, including the set up and if necessary, they will work on their alignment, posture or any element that may be causing issues. As mentioned previously, the fundamentals are certainly not something that apply purely to early starters of the game and are ideally not to be neglected from that point on.

A solvable problem in the set up may very well bring resolution to an issue at the top of the backswing or at impact, for example. This is never 100% guaranteed but understanding the concept will help to reinforce the importance of taking time within the set up and will also allow you to relax a little and have a clearer point of focus without worrying that once you improve one area of the swing you will then have to work on, and fix several others. This is where guidance from your Golf Professional is your first port of call. Your professional is there to help you focus on the most important areas in your swing which may need some attention. It can become a frustrating challenge to try to work things out alone or through the aid of a well meaning playing partner! Often what you feel is an issue within your swing is simply a compensation or reaction to a position or movement that has happened a little earlier on, i.e. feeling difficulty in transferring weight through impact. The brain is an extremely clever part of our anatomy and it will always find a compensatory movement in order to hit the ball as successfully as possible whilst maintaining the body's balance points. If we try to work on the compensatory movement in isolation without tackling the root cause, it can sometimes feel an extremely frustrating process. The fewer compensatory movements the body has to make within your golf swing the easier and more repeatable the movement becomes. The more simplified the motion and the more we can rely on natural forces the easier it is to repeat, particularly under pressure.

So the solution or 'Magic Answer' does not necessarily rest in one 'Magic Move' that works for all but in gaining a simplified understanding of *your* swing and the **primary** solution that creates a positive impact on the ball flight and potentially any sequence that follows. This enables you to simplify your focus, gain trust in what you are working on and encourages a self reliant understanding of your swing, minimising the temptation of never ending experimentation.

Coaching and taking personal responsibility

With regards to taking golf lessons, feeling confident in the understanding of what you are working on and that you feel reasonably self-reliant whilst practising alone is vital to gaining positive long-term results. All good coaches will ensure that this happens. However, taking personal responsibility will strengthen the results. Knowing you have to attain a certain position either in the set up or swing itself, but not having a simplified understanding as to why or what effects it may have on the ball flight has a tendency to create the frustrating loop mentioned previously. If things start to go awry when working alone and unsupervised by a coach, the temptation to experiment creeps in.

With the understanding in place, the way it is put into practice is also vital. Effective practice is pivotal to your improvement. You might feel cheated having spent hours on the driving range, baskets of balls, hands red raw but showing little or no progress. The secret lies in the **quality** of the practice session not the quantity.

Tips for successful practice sessions

Effective practice when working on a swing change, new feeling/movement

Here are a few key tips to successful practice when undergoing any swing changes or implementing new feelings into your swing - It is worth noting that some form of short physical warm up for the body prior to any form of practice session is also greatly beneficial. Some great exercises can be found by visiting www.mytpi.com

• When working on a new feeling/movement, start initially with a mid-iron, 7 or 8 to build up confidence. It's tempting to see if changes will implement themselves straight away with the distance clubs such as the driver or fairway woods but the longer the club the more it has the tendency to highlight any issue if you are slightly out of position at impact. This is not great for confidence levels and delays creating trust in the new movement. Also a club with a lower degree of loft will generally impart more side spin to any shots that are not struck correctly at impact. Once confidence and consistency are gained with the short and mid-irons, gradually work up towards the longer clubs. Also when less emphasis is placed on distance there is a greater opportunity to focus on the quality of the new movement/feeling. Very often distance will be the natural by-product once changes have been confidently established.

• Place the ball on a small tee peg in the early stages of developing a new movement in order to build confidence and trust in any new feelings or positions. It also helps to take away the worry of trying to get the ball airborne and places greater focus on trusting the new movement/feeling. Imagine learning to ride a bike as a small child, using the small stabiliser wheels to start with. If these were taken away too soon the child would fall off, get back on again, fall off, get back on again and so on until eventually all confidence would be lost and it would not be fun anymore.

Picture the tee peg having the same effect. Once you feel confident in repeating the new movement successfully, remove the tee peg and get used to the new movement hitting the ball from the turf/practice mat. The best golfers in the world will still use the aid of a small tee peg whilst initially ingraining a new move or feeling into their swing, often during their non competitive, off season periods.

• Focus on the quality rather than the quantity. Hitting a smaller quantity of balls during shorter more frequent practice sessions rather than a large volume of balls potentially on a more sporadic basis will ensure greater focus and quality is dedicated to each shot.

• Spend time working on any drills your professional may have given you. Often drills that do not involve hitting a ball but recreate the new move or feeling you are working on, benefit your progress greatly. Generally, when a ball is there a greater tendency is to want to trust the old habit no matter how much the brain knows intellectually what needs to be changed. In removing the ball during certain drills or practice routines the mind and body will be more open to trusting a new feeling.

• Create a disciplined routine of correct alignment during your practice session. Place a club or cane on the ground aligned with your chosen target. Once you feel comfortable in repeating the new move and you are gaining repetitive consistency, start to vary your target and vary your club selection, creating a more real life scenario of being out on the golf course. Once the changes are confidently in place, at least some portion of your practice session should replicate the focus and situations you would face on the golf course; this means changing your club and targets every shot or couple of shots and also imagining yourself on a certain hole on the golf course. Simply hitting the same club to the same target throughout the whole of your practice session on the range may feel great at the time; however, it is not fully preparing you for what lies ahead on the golf course.

• They say a picture paints a thousand words and with this in mind using a mirror can be a great learning aid when you are practising. Often a driving range or practice facility will have a bay that has a mirror positioned either in front of you, behind the target line or ideally both. Even working on certain drills and positions at home using a mirror can be highly beneficial. Often what you feel you are doing is not actually what is happening in reality as the old habit tends to be the familiar and most prominent in the early stages of change, hence a visual check provides great feedback. Something as simple as working on your posture in front of a mirror at home for a few minutes a day can provide great benefits and be more fruitful than countless hours firing golf balls on the range.

• Enjoy your practice session. Approaching it with toil, effort and struggle is less likely to produce the results you were hoping for. Take your time, enjoy the challenge, create variety and make it fun!

Effective practice for a pre round warm up

When practising prior to a round purely to warm up, an alternative routine, specific to the round ahead, would be more suitable. The following tips would be advisable:

- Ensure that a pre round warm up session begins with the short game/clubs first, working up to the longer clubs to finish the session.

- If you have a limited amount of time, maybe 10 or 15 minutes, spend it wisely building up feel and timing by pitching, chipping and putting rather than purely hitting shots that are based on distance, avoid rushing to the range solely with the intent of hitting your driver.

- Ideally also include blocks of target specific practice, hitting a repetition of balls with the same club to the same target, blended with variable targets, hitting balls to multiple targets with different clubs. This combination will enable a sound repetition of movement, developing feel, rhythm, timing and confidence along with also re enacting similar scenarios to the ones you will find out on the golf course.

Short Game

- Practice Drill: Up and Down Scramble - This is a great short game exercise. Take 9 balls (fewer quantities of balls may also be used) and scatter them around the green in various positions. Some may land in the rough, some on a sloping lie. Chip or pitch each one on to the green and putt out. Keep your score and each time you do the exercise aim to beat the previous score. The emphasis is on recreating the focus and situation you would find yourself in on the golf course. A degree of repetitive/block practice is great to develop technique and consistency in both contact and distance control. However to then build on this, an exercise that provides variation and on course simulation helps to instil confidence during the round as the scenario has been recreated several times before in practice.

• Take yourself out of your comfort zone and practice the shots you have the tendency to avoid. As golfers, when we are on the range or short game area, we often practice the shots we like and feel more comfortable with! On the golf course we will encounter all manner of shots hence it is beneficial to have put these into practice beforehand. If it is the shorter pitch shot rather than a full swing with the wedge, be sure to blend these into the practice session. If you are still finding difficulty with these shots consider seeking guidance from your professional, any form of attention and TLC given to this area of the game, the all important 'scoring zone' will definitely reap its rewards! (This will also be discussed in a little more detail in later chapters).

THE KEY TO BECOMING YOUR OWN BEST COACH

Really good teachers, teach you how to teach yourself' – Jack Nicklaus

Enabling students to become as self-reliant as possible has always been a key goal of mine from a coaching perspective. I believe a huge influence on allowing this to happen, as mentioned previously, comes from each golfer having a basic understanding of their **own** individual game and swing. Of course this process may be a little more gradual for complete newcomers to the game. The statement may then be raised 'I don't need to know the why's, just tell me what to do!' This is certainly one approach and by no means is it to imply or encourage getting overly analytical about things, however, if you want to make improvements, and for them to be sustainable over a long period of time, it helps to have a degree of self sufficiency in the form of a basic understanding of **your** golf swing/movement and its correlation to the motion of the ball. If you are working on something technically in your golf swing, ideally through the aid of professional guidance, **it needs to make logical sense to you.** With this comes the faith that will enable you to trust it and gain greater sustained success. If there lies any doubt or there is a sense of having to work on a certain movement or feeling but not really knowing why, simply going through the motions with a degree of uncertainty, the temptation of experimenting with several alternative theories if things start to falter slightly greatly increases.

> *'You only change what you understand. What you do not understand and are not aware of, you don't change. But when you understand it, it changes.'*
> *Anthony De Mello*

Empowering yourself to be your own coach

To truly empower and fulfil your potential on a consistent and long term basis it can be extremely beneficial for each golfer to have a degree of understanding of the following two aspects:

a) **Why** the ball is reacting as it is, and what, in your swing, is the *primary* cause

b) **Why** you are working on a certain position or movement in your swing and how this will affect and impact the motion of the ball.

I want to stress here once again that it is not an encouragement to over think or analyse your golf swing but a simple understanding which will prevent that roller coaster ride of searching and experimentation.

Let's describe it other terms: **cause and effect**.

If you can understand the main root cause in your golf swing that is having any undesired effect on the golf ball, you are in a much more powerful position than second guessing several different areas in your swing and experimenting with different concepts or swing thoughts. I am not denying that these concepts may be extremely sound advice in their own right, but in relation to your swing they may not apply, and only send you onto the golf course feeling more confused and frustrated. The beauty is that very often, as stated earlier, addressing the key area in need of some attention can have a positive chain reaction on the following sequence or sequences; you don't always have to then over analyse, perfect or break down each segment of the golf swing.

When things suddenly go wrong!

There are sometimes days when it literally feels as though an alien has come in and completely invaded your golf swing, panic sets in and you think drastic changes have happened over night and you now have to fix these additional issues! To put your mind at rest, this rarely happens. Often golfers natural tendencies and patterns of movement become habitual, it is fairly rare that a new, destructive element inserts itself into the golf swing over night or even from shot to shot! Golf would become an extremely challenging game if we swung the club differently every time we stood up to the ball. Rest assured, although at times, it may feel as though this happens, it is often a similar pattern of movement to a lesser or greater degree, the change generally stemming from an increase in tension and or change of timing. Granted there may be situations where an aspect of the fundamentals, as an example, may have gradually slipped out of position but rarely does something dramatic happen overnight!

During a coaching session and following on from an explanation about an aspect within the swing that may require a little work, if a shot goes awry often the question is asked 'What did I do there?'. Again nothing happened differently from that which had been explained initially, it just may have happened to a greater or lesser extent. In addition, the rhythm and timing of the swing might have altered the feeling and result quite significantly, but the actual movement often remains the same. If you understand this and you understand the ***basic*** concept of your own golf swing, not in an overly technical way, it is less likely that panic will surface during any potential 'off' periods. There is also less inclination to search for that missing 'secret' hidden in the multitude of golfing archives!

When we reduce any excess tension we can also begin to gain an awareness of the weight of the club head and in turn a greater awareness of where the club head is during the golf swing. With solid fundamentals in place within the set up it then becomes easier to allow natural forces to assist in creating a more simplified motion. From a relatively good set up position generally natural forces will not force the club into unnatural or extreme positions. In developing greater feel and awareness of the club head within the swing it also enables a sense of self sufficiency and more intrinsic control over our games and development. Ironically it is in fact a feeling of letting go along with an element of trust that gives us more control as oppose to feeling as though we need to control the golf club throughout each moment of the swing. Relying on external feedback, i.e. using training aids, can help with development up to a point however it is important they are not relied on consistently over long periods of time as this can make it difficult to transition and feel self sufficient once the aid has been removed and when out on the golf course.

Developing a basic understanding of the golf swing

Having an incorrect conceptual understanding of the basics of the golf swing as a whole can also lead to years of frustration. A simple switch in your understanding can transform everything in an instant, without any technical trials or tribulations. Here is an example: For 30 plus years, a pupil had played golf with that all too common left to right slice on the ball (as a right handed golfer). He had been taking lessons, working hard and grinding away in an effort to eliminate the right hand side of the golf course. His instructor at the time asked what his understanding of the golf swing was in his own mind. He explained that he thought the golf swing worked as a straight line. He had focused on taking the club back on a straight line for as long as he could in the backswing, having read about a wide takeaway, and the same on the follow through. His instructor then began to explain that, in fact, the golf swing worked more along the lines of a circular motion, and that only the very initial part of the takeaway and backswing actually worked along a straight line. Yes a degree of width in the takeaway is important but if over emphasised, could have a detrimental impact. The minute this was impressed on the mind of the pupil he instantly and naturally made changes, including his posture, to accommodate the new understanding he had. After a few shots, he promptly produced his best ball flight in 30 years; the slice had dissolved purely through eradicating his misperception of how he thought the golf swing ought to be. He didn't even have to think how to do it, the new understanding shifted things naturally. This example highlights the impact any misperceptions held may have on a golfer's progress.

Keeping your head down is arguably one of the most commonly heard solutions to all golfing woes, yet this concept, unfortunately if misunderstood, can be just as detrimental as is beneficial. Yes the head wants to remain steady during the swing, i.e. maintaining relatively the same height throughout the swing, however if held down excessively, to the point where the body is unable to rotate efficiently, contact, accuracy and distance can all be compromised and suffer as a consequence.

Let's use an analogy in another learning context. As a youngster, I have to admit, when it came to maths, algebra and fractions, I wasn't the brightest cookie in the jar! I found it a struggle, to say the least.

The key underlying issue was based around the fact that I didn't have the basic understanding of the formula. Instead, I simply tried to wade through the problem with a bit of memory recall mixed with a dash of luck and hope, without really knowing how to solve it. If there were ten questions, luck and memorising by parrot fashion would maybe get me through the easy first two or three, however the remaining 70% became a complete hit and miss scenario as I did not fully understand the underlying process behind the question. I could get away with the very easy ones but it would not transpire across the board. With additional help of a personal tutor, I learned that I was actually making things much more complicated than I needed to and with his simplified explanation and a greater understanding I passed with flying colours! This is exactly where the maths tutor and golf professional actually share the very same role – to help students understand the key basics and correct concept to enable greater self sustainability. The golf swing does not in any way want to be compared to a complex maths equation. However, it does help to highlight the advantages of having a basic understanding of the fundamentals of the golf swing and the correct basic concepts.

Consider this scenario: If you have an excessively rounded spine in your posture and set up, predominantly caused through bending from the stomach/neck rather than hinging from the hips, the opportunity to turn or rotate becomes more limited. A relatively straight spine creates a simple axis to rotate around. It makes logical sense that you would potentially need to pull up/lift your spine/head at some point in order to compensate or overcome the limitations of a rounded spine during the swing. The basic concept is – Relatively straight spine = easy rotation, Rounded spine = compensatory move i.e. lifting the head/body.

If we simply think about keeping our head down or try to memorise a posture position without any understanding or reasoning, it inevitably becomes much more of an inconsistent process. There is a far greater chance of giving up on something if it feels a little awkward when we don't understand the reasoning behind it and its impact. A simple understanding brings greater and sustainable ease.

Awkward and sloping lies can also be used as another great example and is an area that can create confusion or uncertainty for many golfers. The importance of understanding the 'whys', as mentioned in the previous chapter, are of great benefit when learning the basic principles of playing a shot from a less than perfect lie. There are normally four basic sloping lies on the golf course. These are:

- Ball above the feet
- Ball below the feet
- Uphill lie
- Downhill lie

Each of these sloping lies require different adjustments to be made as the lie of the land will affect the set up, swing and ball flight in slightly different ways.

Principles for managing sloping lies

Several set up principles may change according to the relevant slope. You may conclude that this requires memorising multiple adjustments for the four different lies/slopes. I often think back to the look of panic in golfers eyes when they worry that they have to memorise each of these - they feel the urgency to grab a piece of paper and pen before they forget!

The thought of needing to memorise a multitude of different positions with regards to slopes on the golf course is a little like trying to memorise twenty different mathematical equations (from my algebra example earlier). Without the understanding behind the formula it becomes reliant on memory recall and often becomes an inconsistent and unreliable plan of attack. I believe there is an easier option and that simply comes through a **simplified** understanding of some of the 'whys'.

Understanding the whys versus memory recall

Let's take the example of 'ball above your feet'. The slope itself encourages a flatter motion and swing plane (the degree of which will depend on the severity of the slope), creating more hands and arm rotation through the shot and causing the clubface to close down at a faster rate on the downswing.

This combined with the slope changing the way the club sits on the ground during the set up and encouraging the loft of the club to aim to the left means that the ball may travel to the left in the air (for a right handed golfer). In this scenario having a basic understanding enables things to embed themselves a little more rather than purely trying to memorise various positions. The severity of the slope and each golfer's natural ball flight also come into play however in this instance the key factor is the simplified understanding. (Sloping lie pointers can also be found in the end notes at the rear of the book)

The concept of loosely linking some of the similarities between the various sloping lies combined with a simplified understanding allows it to become a process that ultimately feels like common sense, rather than a panic of memory recall, this in turn creates greater sustainability and consistency. Understanding the basic concepts will also allow you to play the shot in greater confidence. There is nothing worse than approaching a shot with tension and panic as a result of being unsure of how to play it. Where sloping lies are concerned anxiety and tension can potentially cause the body to work in opposition to gravity and natural forces purely through fearing the outcome and trying to control the shot. (Fear of outcome will be addressed in a later chapter). Having a vague memory of 'I think the ball should be forward in the stance, I'm not sure why but will give it a go!' may come up trumps now and then, but when you know for sure what to do, because you understand the reasons why and its impact, you can commit fully, allowing you to channel your energy and focus confidently into the shot at hand.

The captain of your ship!

Each golfer holds the potential to become a much more self-reliant player on a more consistent and long term basis. In order to master the art of becoming your own coach it helps significantly to gain a simplistic understanding of *your* swing and game as a whole. Combine a clear understanding of any areas you may be working on with a sound conceptual understanding of the golf swing and a trust in your own natural instincts, and you are well on your way to being the captain of your own ship. If the seas become a little choppy every now and then, you know exactly what to do to steer your way through to calmer waters! This does not mean you won't ever need or want professional assistance ever again beyond that point; it simply means you will feel a greater confidence, self reliance and in turn, a greater consistency and level of success without continually seeking out the latest 'Money back guarantee golf fix!' Ultimately, all good coaches worth their weight, whether it be in sport, business, education or life wants their student to become self sufficient, confident and to flourish in the long term. A coach is not there to act as a crutch; needed each and every single moment something goes wrong. This rarely provides long term satisfaction or results, and can at the very least become rather expensive! A coach is there to guide, inspire and support, acting as a tour guide to unearth the true potential that lies in every student. Find a coach you can trust, one who empowers you to become self reliant through a simple understanding of your own game, one who enables you to gain a sound understanding of the fundamentals and one who understands your needs fully as an individual, expanding your strengths and developing any areas that may benefit from improvement.

> ***'Educating is not a process of directing instruction, but to inspire, to feed curiosity, to facilitate'* – Sir Ken Robinson.**

THE TECHNOLOGY OF COACHING

'Absorb what is useful, discard what is not, add what is uniquely yours' – *Bruce Lee*

Modern day golf technology is forever on the increase and its opportunities for progress are fantastic with endless possibilities available at our fingertips. From a coaching perspective the technology available can certainly assist greatly in providing a more precise and in depth look at the technical elements of the golf swing, biomechanics and ball flight data. However, for the golfer it is important to feel comfortable in knowing at which point the seemingly endless information that technology provides begins to outweigh its benefits. Relative to the ability level of the golfer, how much knowledge is too much and at what point does the balance of information overload versus benefit tip the scales?

Today's golfing technology

Let's consider some of the options currently available on the market today:

Radar Technology - launch monitors/simulators – These devices can assess many different parameters of what is happening to the ball flight, as well as monitor the club delivery, including club head speed, swing path, swing plane, angle of attack and many more. One particular brand of launch monitor, Trackman, produces approximately twenty-six different pieces of data per ball struck. The question is, for the average golfer, how much of that information does he or she really need to know?

The first consideration is the level of ability. The elite amateur and professional may find some of the additional data and statistics a little more beneficial, providing a positive impact to their game. For the club golfer, however, too much data can potentially be detrimental to their progress. This piece of equipment can be used for both coaching purposes, as well as club fitting and analyzing the efficiency of current equipment, and/or purchasing of new.

Let's look at the instance of club fitting.

If the launch monitor is being used for fitting purposes and new equipment, then potentially only a handful (three or four) of the twenty six pieces of data available would be of key importance. This may vary slightly from person to person but on the whole it effectively reduces the available data down quite dramatically! Is there a benefit in golfers gaining insight into each and every one of those figures, in my professional opinion, no. Can a selection of those figures when professionally filtered assist in progress, absolutely.

Where equipment is concerned in its most simple form, it boils down to the question '**Is this club working for me or against me?**' There are many marketing strategies that promise extra yardage or anti slice remedies, to name a few, and yes they can provide gains, albeit sometimes marginal. However, when it comes to deciding on whether to buy new equipment and what to buy, the initial priority lies in assessing whether what you are currently using is optimising your game or whether it is in fact detrimental in some form. Ideally your equipment wants to assist in optimising and dovetailing with your physiology, ability and golf swing.

Some key priorities lie in weight, length, lie angle, shaft flex and clubhead design/forgiveness. If these are not working for you, the game can become a much greater challenge. Here is a relatively simplified example which I have witnessed fairly frequently: A mid to high handicap golfer with a slightly slower than average swing speed has been having problems with their driver, predominantly with tee shots drifting to the right (as a right handed golfer) and feeling as though distance is diminishing. They have been loaned a club to try by a well-meaning friend in an attempt to resolve the issue! It has a stiff, relatively heavy shaft, with 9.5 degrees of loft and is the latest club on the market promising great gains in accuracy and distance!

This driver may be the latest, most advanced and expensive club freshly out on the market however it is potentially not working in an advantageous fashion for this particular golfer, regardless of what it promises in terms of distance, technology or rewards. Unfortunately, without the knowledge and understanding of this, persistence in trying to stick with it can begin to greatly affect confidence levels and potentially knock the swing further out of kilter. One in ten shots may work reasonably well, however relying on only a 10% chance of success can make the game feel like a frustrating uphill struggle. Selecting a club with a combination of elements which enable you to hit successful shots the greater percentage of time even when you don't put your best swing on the ball is the ideal solution. It's a hard one to swallow sometimes but in golf *'Consistency is better than rare moments of greatness!'* There are times of course where addressing the technicalities of the swing may bring greater gains from a consistency point of view, however it is important to ensure the equipment is complimenting and making the most of a golfers technique and physiology rather than hindering.

The key to equipment is to make life easy for yourself and allow the club to work for you. *Allow* the shaft to work for you effortlessly, don't try to **make** a shaft work for you. *Allow* the weight of the club let you generate your maximum clubhead speed potential when you put a comfortable swing on the ball, not when you give it your all. *Allow* the length of the club let you hit shots consistently and accurately, yet provide the desired distance within those parameters. Select the clubhead that assists you in creating your desired ball flight

80% of the time rather than fighting to find the sweet spot 20% of the time. Choose the loft that assists you in creating the optimal launch angle and trajectory for you. The common theme to all of the above factors is to find a club which **allows you to put a reasonable swing on the ball and still provides a greater average of consistency** rather than having to generate your very best swing to gain your best shot only a small percentage of the time. This is where technology, with the aid of a professional, can help as it provides data highlighting the optimum average figures for you and in turn the club that is right for you, not necessarily what you feel you ought to be using. It also helps to reduce the temptation of selecting a club which appears as though it produces your best shot but on an irregular basis.

The key to using the data offered by ball flight monitors, and in fact all forms of coaching technology, lies in the quality and relevance of the information and not the quantity. We have highlighted the club fitting scenario above, however the importance of data interpretation of course also applies when having a golf lesson. The coach is there to decipher the most relevant piece or pieces of data for you and your golf swing.

Other technology and its benefits

Other forms of current coaching technology lie in video analysis, biomechanical feedback systems, putting analysers and balance plates which analyse weight distribution throughout the swing. These are all fantastic pieces of equipment. However they too have the potential to flood the golfer with information, figures and statistics. For the average golfer, once again, the key to maximising their benefits lies in acquiring the relevant **filtered** knowledge from a trained professional. This will provide the most direct route to improvement.

One of the greatest benefits of this fantastic technology lies in its ability to provide information which the naked eye has absolutely no way of physically capturing. Prior to the introduction of Trackman and other forms of launch monitors, many coaches, myself included, worked on the premise that the club path - the direction the club travels into impact, held the greatest influence on the initial starting direction of the golf ball. My early years of training were certainly based on this concept. Scientific data has proven this theory incorrect and in fact it is the club face that has the greatest influence on the initial starting direction of the golf ball at impact. It was discovered that the face angle on the driver accounts for roughly 85% of the initial direction and for irons the face angle accounts for around 75%. The human eye would have no way of acquiring these figures, facts and sources of data.

This reliable data not only provides a detailed and concrete evidence base for the professional, but most importantly instils a confidence and faith in the information being relayed from the coach to pupil, either in what they may be working on technically or in a particular club; this is worth its weight in gold. If any doubt lies within the pupil, either questioning whether a golf club is right for them or in what they may be working on technically in their golf swing, there can be a temptation to experiment in alternatives. Technology provides the evidence-based data to assist in binding the faith not only within the pupil, but also between pupil and coach. It instils a confidence and commitment to the process and helps to prevent the inconsistent and frustrating journey of experimentation.

When used with a degree of consistency, devices such as launch monitors can also provide a detailed positive reference point for what is happening in the golfers swing when they are playing well, the ideal optimal to strive towards when playing at their best. Not only utilising generic recommended stats as a comparison but their very own personal reference point for when *they* play at their best as an individual. This also creates a positive focal point and a confidence in the achievable. Often we look to technology to guide us when we feel things aren't going so well but it can be just as important to be aware of what is happening when we are playing well. Professionals will very often collate data during the times in their season when they are playing their best providing feedback to refer back to when needed. I use the term reference point as I also believe it is important not to become solely reliant on stats and numbers. Ensuring the golfer maintains self reliance through the development of feel and a sound yet simplified understanding of their own golf swing is also key.

Modern day technology is now becoming available whereby statistical analysis of the swing and ball flight can be made on a self-reliant basis through devices which can be attached to a club or golf glove and utilised by the golfer directly, either on the range, putting green or comfort of their own home, without having a golf lesson or the assistance of a trained professional. This may provide beneficial data to the golfer; however, misinterpretation of this data can impart greater confusion and frustration. Data, in this instance, is only as valuable as its interpretation. From a coaching perspective, I would always recommend when using such devices that an initial evaluation be carried out under the guidance of a professionally trained eye. Once you have the correct interpretation of the data, and an understanding of the most relevant pieces of information to you, they become a much more beneficial companion.

> *'Radar technology defines clubhead speed, the launch angle and spin rates of our shots, but it cannot measure strength of spirit'* – *Thomas Bjorn*

ELIMINATING THE DESTRUCTIVE

'Golf is about how well you accept, respond to, and score with your misses much more so than it is a game of your perfect shots' – Dr Bob Rotella

The key to consistent golf is **not** necessarily to create the perfect golf swing and strike each ball directly out of the centre very time. Of course it feels great if this does happen, however, even the most experienced and talented professionals do not attain this day in day out, shot after shot. A four round tournament is not necessarily won through perfectly struck shots but through **minimising any destruction.** What the best golfers in the world do, the ones who are consistently in the top 10 rankings, is build on their strengths and acknowledge and minimise any destructive element. Combining this with a sound mind-set is certainly on the right track to a winning combination!

How to eliminate the destructive

The first step is to acknowledge your strengths and also what area of your game or specific shot, if there is one, gets you into any difficulty; this will vary from person to person. This is not to berate yourself or place all of your focus on the negative. However, simply be aware of a key area that with some amendments may make the biggest difference in a positive way to your game. It also does not mean having to make everything perfect or make a major re-haul. Whether it is a pull hook off the tee when the stakes are high, those short 3ft putts, a 40 yard pitch, or a shot, which on a windy day takes you into the depths of no return, acknowledge it and begin to make the positive changes to *minimise* its destruction, note minimise, not perfect!

Secondly, at times, a great deal of energy can be frustratingly spent focussing on the wrong areas. The main priority is to reduce any destructive element, which in turn will begin to make the biggest and quickest impact on your score. An unplayable ball out of bounds turned into a shot finishing in the light rough will put you in a far better position of recovery, reducing the chance of any high numbers on that hole. In this example (in the case of a right handed golfer) it isn't necessary to try to perfect the ball flight into a subtle draw or even a perfectly straight shot, but simply reduce the amount of left to right movement on the ball which will consistently bring it back into play, rather than having to reload after a lost ball each time. It may even be a pitch shot that consistently gives you a chance of putting rather than having to chip back from the other side of the green each time. Each golfer's situation will potentially differ quite dramatically, however the solution to greater consistency will remain the same.

It doesn't require a painstaking remodelling of several different parts of your golf swing or game, but simply understanding and pinpointing the key underlying element that causes your troublesome shot, improving it and reducing its detrimental impact. If you can find the primary root cause that will reduce any destructive shot in your bag, you are well on your way to finding that consistency. Don't be concerned with perfecting every aspect, simply identify the key area for you and in doing so a positive ripple effect on your game overall will generally follow.

Let's use an example. A commonly heard tip within the golf swing is to keep your left arm straight (for a right handed golfer). You have noticed that your left arm folds very slightly in your backswing and consider that this may be the cause of your pull hook off the tee. You read a great article about the importance of a straight left arm, you then spend a great deal of time trying to straighten the arm, increasing the tension, but to no avail, you feel frustrated and confused. Yes, ideally the left arm wants to be comfortably straight, however there may be something much more significant that is causing your troublesome shot and there may even be something a little earlier on that encourages that slight fold as a compensatory move. The more you focus on trying to keep the left arm poker straight, the more tension is created and ultimately it is not necessarily the root cause of the problem. A lot of time and energy may have been frustratingly wasted.

Relax – everything doesn't have to be perfect!

Ultimately, relax in the knowledge that everything doesn't have to be perfect to make notable differences in your game, in either the shots you play or your golf swing. For the quickest results, simply pin point and acknowledge, in a **constructive yet positive light**, any shot, which on a reasonably consistent basis, gets you into difficulty on the golf course. Locate the primary source causing the issue, and work towards an improvement whether that be bringing the ball back into play, a bunker shot that gives you a chance to putt rather than yet another bunker shot or a 4 putt that becomes 2, whichever it may be, the end result will be a much more consistent scorecard with less frustration on the way. Of course, mindset can also be a component when discussing a potentially destructive or troublesome element within your game and also plays a vital role in how we respond to it; however this will be discussed in later chapters.

As mentioned, many of the world's top golfers lead by example in terms of minimising any destructive element in their game. They need to minimise their errors where a four-round tournament is concerned. One or two blow-up holes during a round can take them from the top 10 on day one to missing the cut after day two. One player that springs to mind is multiple major tournament winner and one of golf's greats, Lee Trevino. Trevino during his prime had a unique style of his own. Not necessarily text book or traditionally orthodox, however his success came from knowing his own game, maximising his strengths and minimising any destruction that would take him out of contention during a four-round tournament. He did not worry about trying to turn his natural left to right ball flight into a perfectly straight shot; he played to his strengths, eliminated any destructive element and had a hugely successful career in the process. He also had a great reputation for enjoying himself on the golf course, all in all, not a bad formula to emulate!

Yes there are ideals to aim for from a technical and ball flight perspective and yes, everybody wants to hit the centre of the clubface and fairway as often as possible or wants the ball to finish a few inches from the pin. This is not to say these are not attainable by any means. However, if, as an example, replacing a shot out of bounds with the finishing in light rough means potentially saving 2 or 3 shots on a hole, this is your initial focal point and most direct route to consistent success.

From a coaching perspective I have often experienced working with students whereby the margins of error on a particular shot have improved dramatically to the point where the opportunity of getting the ball around the golf course successfully has greatly improved. There still however, lies a little disappointment in them as they feel the perfect shot, in their eyes, is just out of reaching distance, there may still, as an example, be a little side spin remaining on the ball. The key aim however, is ultimately damage limitation. When improvements have been made that enable the ball to remain consistently in play or where destructive elements have been minimised and this is reflective in the score, this must be positively acknowledged and embraced. Building on strengths and **minimising** any destructive elements will enable you to **consistently** improve how you score and get the golf ball around the golf course.

QUICK FIX VERSUS LONG TERM DEVELOPMENT

'The road reaches every place, the short cut only one ' – *James Richardson*

All golfers are unique and individual. Golfers also differ in how they learn, not only in how they take on board information (visual, kinaesthetic, auditory), but also in their learning preferences, what they want to get from their game and ultimately their end goals. Every golfer wants to feel they have an opportunity for improvement and it can be a natural instinct to want to improve as quickly as possible. This is completely understandable and there is no rule saying there is anything wrong with this. However, it does raise the question, 'can I improve instantly with a quick fix, or do I opt for a longer term plan of development?'

Quick fix versus long-term development: what are the differences?

Both options will give the golfer a solution. However, the **key differences lie in how long will the solutions last.** A quick fix is generally a tweak within some aspect of the set up or swing that will potentially create a cure for the near future, the next round or competition, or maybe a little longer. There is absolutely no problem with this, providing it comes with the understanding that it **may** be temporary.

Quite often a quick fix is offering a compensation for a fundamental issue potentially happening elsewhere in the golf swing, it acts as a band-aid on the effect rather than targeting the root cause. There is no denying that there are times when a small tweak is all that is needed to provide some relief and improvement within your game, even if it simply provides a lift in confidence and enjoyment. However if you are finding that under pressure the same problem shot consistently gets you into trouble, the band-aid unfortunately, at some point, may give way and the quick fix option may not be the best solution.

A long-term approach provides the opportunity of bringing lasting results and a better understanding of your game as a whole. This alternative option can, however, sometimes seem slightly less appealing. There is often a misperception that the swing must be completely broken down and remodelled with months of frustration, painstaking hours on the range and involves taking a huge step backwards before going forwards. This doesn't have to be the case. Your professional will of course be instrumental in helping you through the process. Where possible, try not to be swayed by the well-meaning advice of your playing partners as this will potentially extend progress time. In the long-run, repetitive experimentation without the help of a coach may drag improvement out further.

'Long term development', doesn't have to mean long term, as in the time it takes to improve. Yes it may require a little more time than the quick fix, however, adopting the longer term development approach enables you to identify the root cause of any issue, gain an understanding of your swing, its correlation to the ball flight/contact and develop the most effective practice plan for your needs. It is worth noting that **effective practice** also plays an integral role in speedy development. Part of your long-term development may also involve using a more holistic approach, assessing fitness, mind-set and any areas in need of change to help support development. Ultimately 'long term' means an approach that will provide consistent results further down the line and assist in achieving greater success when faced under pressure.

Owing to the uniqueness of each golfer and with each wanting different things from their game and their methods of progress, both options, quick fix and long-term, are widely available. There is not necessarily a right or wrong, the key lies in understanding and acknowledging how each operate and what they can offer to your game. With this knowledge brings free will and the choice of personal preference.

ONE SIZE FITS ALL – OR DOES IT?!

'In order to be irreplaceable, one must always be different' – Coco Chanel

In modern day coaching, many swing styles and models are read about, talked about and studied via the various media sources. For example, you may have heard of the Stack and Tilt, One Plane, Two Plane and so on. Reading and hearing about different swing models and approaches to the golf swing can become a little confusing as you think about which one is the ideal or which one should you opt for if you feel you are currently not happy with your progress. We know performance does not rely on technique alone; however the key is that each model in its own right will have its benefits and reasons why you should work towards that particular style. **The single most important rule of thumb is that it must suit you as an individual** and blend with your current style, ability and physical make up. It can become catastrophic to completely change your swing simply to fit into the current model or swing style that is in the 'spotlight' at that particular moment in time. Some of the best golfers in the world have tried to adapt or change their swing to work towards a certain swing style or model with poor results; it simply did not suit or blend with their own natural swing pattern and/or physiology. This is not to play down in any way the theory and benefits of that particular model, it may however not be the best option based on a golfers current method, style and physicality. This may be a difficult obstacle or decision to overcome alone and with professional guidance it can be established as to which options may be the most suitable for you, remembering that everyone is very different as an individual and does not have to slot into one way of swinging the golf club.

Basic principles: Biomechanical sequence and physiology

Of course there are some basic principles that apply to being able to hit consistently good golf shots. I am not suggesting there are several different efficient impact positions. Through the aid of modern day technology we are aware of the basic principles that produce optimal impact and the optimal efficient body sequencing required biomechanically. All good ball strikers are very similar in reproducing these optimal parameters. However there may be several options and preferences of how to reach that point. We know that biomechanically, all of the best ball strikers on the Professional Tour will swing the golf club in the same efficient sequence in the start of the down swing: Feet, lower body/pelvis, thorax, arms and club. If we start to rearrange this sequence in any way when aiming to produce distance and accuracy within a full swing there could be disastrous results, depending on how the sequence is altered.

With regards to the physiology of a golfer, physical limitations may influence how a player adopts or favours certain positions. It may not be ideal to then try to mould that player into an alternative set model.

How unorthodox swings can work so well

Within a successful golf swing, where it appears a little unorthodox, one movement will match its opposition to allow for the best possible results at impact. This reflects Newton's 3rd law - every action has an equal and opposite reaction. If something in the swing is changed and produces a mismatch of movements, results may be potentially poor. You may see a few slightly unorthodox looking swings within the best players in the world, the key however, is that the efficient body sequencing is the same as a conventional swing with compensatory movements to promote an efficient impact position. The biomechanics and internal efficient engine are generally the same.

Jim Furyk is a fine example. One of the world's top money earning players on tour may not have the most text book of swings from an external point of view, however aside from a solid mental focus and a good short game, technically the following key elements allow him be to as successful as he is:

- Solid fundamentals in the set up
- Efficient body sequencing
- An efficient impact position
- Matching movements in the swing
- Efficient timing

Yes, ideally, the fewer compensations that have to be made during the swing, the better. However, players such as Jim Furyk as an example, who have a relatively unorthodox looking swing, are highly talented individuals and have been grooving the same repetitive movement, often from a very young age and have hit thousands of balls in the process. To mould Jim Furyk into a different model and style from the one he is currently using and one that, although slightly unorthodox, earned him a top ten place for over 430 weeks in the World rankings between 1999 and 2015, I'm not convinced may be the wisest of moves! Ultimately the key is to work with what suits **you** as an individual and allows you to consistently swing the golf club in its most simplified manner, resulting in a consistently efficient impact position and ball strike. One size does not necessarily fit all.

THE POWER SOURCES

'I get as much fun as the next man from whaling the ball as hard as I can and catching it squarely on the button. But from sad experience I learned not to try this in a round that meant anything!' –
Bobby Jones

Distance is a greatly desired word within the golfing world; everybody wants to hit the ball further. Understandably, it is very satisfying to hit the ball a long way. However, when it comes at the expense of consistency and accuracy, it may need rethinking and reassessing. Often the ways in which power is sought after in the golf swing can generate more harm than good. Any attempt to gain extra distance through over exertion of the body, whether that is through tension, incorrect timing or excess body motion can in fact have the reverse effect.

Understanding power in the golf swing

Relaxed state

A relaxed state is potentially not the first thing that springs to a golfers mind when wanting to gain an extra 20 yards on their drive! However, achieving this both physiologically and psychologically can have a profoundly positive impact on your swing, distance and your game as a whole. Excessive physical tension with regards to generating distance can be a huge roadblock. Psychologically, the anxious mind can often be worrying about the undesired outcome and generally brings with it a degree of tension. I will talk more about this in following chapters. However, learning to adopt a relaxed and focussed mind-set will, in turn, generate a more relaxed physiology and a greater opportunity for greater distance to develop through a more relaxed and efficient body motion.

Let's look first of all look at tension within in the grip, a common tendency when wanting to gain those extra yards on your drive!

Keep it light

Excessive grip pressure can be a natural instinct when striving for distance. Unfortunately the tension spreads itself up through the arms, into the shoulders and before you know it the whole of the upper body has become a much more constricted and restricted power source. The upper body, when in a relaxed state, allows the shoulders and chest to open up much more; when tense, the shoulders become generally more rounded and from here it becomes much harder for the upper body to create sufficient and efficient rotation in the backswing, the body almost gets in its own way.

The key is to keep grip pressure relatively light, also allowing for a more relaxed upper body. The body can now work more efficiently and the relaxed grip, can also enable the natural hand action to take place, both in the backswing and allowing the natural release through the impact area and follow through, potentially generating greater clubhead speed. When the hand action becomes inhibited due to tight grip pressure (this can also be contributed to incorrect positioning of the hands on the grip) contact and distance can be greatly affected, two levers in effect become one. Imagine throwing a ball whereby the action is created by utilising just one lever, with little or no hand/wrist action. The chances of gaining distance are diminished and it certainly becomes a greater effort relying on sheer strength. This is exactly the same within the golf swing. Often when the hand/wrist action is limited, in order to get more power and length in the backswing, a second but incorrectly placed lever is added by a fold of the left arm/elbow (for a right handed golfer). The folding of the left arm can become a compensatory movement. Unfortunately trying to then correct it by straightening the arm through increasing the tension simply adds to the problem. In this instance, the frequently used term 'keep your left arm straight' can in fact be of more detriment than benefit. The tighter the grip and arm pressure, the more limited the natural hand/wrist action, the more the left arm potentially folds in order to try and generate power and momentum.

If you imagine a scale numbered 1 – 10 where 1 would be the lightest you could hold the club and 10 the tightest, the half way point at around 5 would be ideal. Try to gain the sensation of the weight of the clubhead, in holding the club too tightly it becomes harder to distinguish the weight of the club head from the overall weight of the club, it almost all feels as one. There will be a sensation of pressure across the fingers (and thumbs) as there still needs to feel a supporting of the golf club however this will feel a different sensation to grasping the club tightly in the palm of the hands.

It may help to give the club a small waggle to release any tension and to assist in gaining greater awareness and a sensation of the weight of the club head. Simply having the awareness of excessive tension is a big step forward. When the upper body is more relaxed it is also able to create a huge power source when it turns efficiently around a relatively stable lower body. This is key.

An efficient body, working from the ground upwards.

All rotary athletes, including the golfer, work from the ground upwards. The legs, gluteal muscles (buttocks) and core abdominal muscles are pivotal for balance as well as for power and stability. The upper body coiling efficiently around a stable base provides a powerful resistance between the two which then uncoils into the downswing releasing effortless power. When attempting to generate power through excessive turning of the body, this resistance is lost.

From a stable set up, aside from the natural knee flex created within the posture, a relatively straight line is formed from your right foot, knee and hip (for a right handed golfer) during your backswing. If either the right hip or knee slides to the outside of the foot or the knee collapses inwards a power source is instantly lost. Power is also lost through a limited turn and of course the very common issue of an over ambitious turn. The hips need only turn approximately half the amount of the shoulders, (i.e. forty degrees hip turn to eighty degrees of shoulder turn) to enable the upper body to coil effectively around the lower body and produce the degree of hip and shoulder turn needed to release effortless power. Excessive movement in the backswing, by tilting, sliding or over-rotating reduces the stability in the lower body and resistance between the upper and lower body. It is the torque generated between the two that creates what is commonly known as the X factor.

One of the world's long driving champions Jason Sadlowski, creates a whopping 117 degrees of X factor; 49 degrees of hip turn and 166 degrees of shoulder turn. I am not suggesting that the average golfer try to match these kinds of figures. In fact, I would issue a warning of, 'Please do not try that at home folks!' However, it does highlight a key factor that plays a significant part in enabling him to hit the ball as far as he does - the separation between his hip turn and shoulder turn. Of course his athletic physique also allows him to achieve such figures. An over-ambitious turn where the hips attempt to turn equal amounts to the shoulders reduces this X factor stretch and power source.

Imagine firing a catapult. Tension is created when the elastic is pulled back from a stable base which is then released to launch the object into the distance. If the stable base followed the elastic or became unstable in any way, very little resistance would be generated and there would be no platform upon which to release and launch the object. The upper and lower body work in exactly the same way during the golf swing when generating distance. Of course everybody is built differently and it is not necessary to create an extreme stretch, forcing the body unhealthily outside of its capabilities. **Simply understanding the benefits of creating a relatively stable lower body, combined with a sufficiently rotated yet relaxed upper body, and generating some separation between the two, will reap its rewards.** Turning the body to an extreme, will not.

It is also worth noting that if physical limitations impede an over-ambitious turn, the body will find an alternative way to complete the backswing. It will find a cheating mechanism, as an example an alternative route may be for the spine and upper body to lift up into the backswing rather than rotate. Compensations will need to follow and consistency, amongst other things, will be lost. A golfer will find it very difficult to maximise club head speed without developing an efficient body motion and ensuring the body can physically support the increased forces.

The lower body and legs are a big power source when used correctly. If we liken an unstable lower body to that of playing golf on ice you can see how the upper body would be forced to tighten and simply react in any which way it can to keep its balance. This is also what happens in the golf swing if the lower body becomes unstable. When the lower body acts as a stable base it allows the body levels to remain relatively constant, providing a much better chance of striking the ball in the same spot each time at impact. It is worth noting that a stable lower body still provides a degree of mobility, the legs and hips do not want to remain completely static, however if excessive movement is made causing changes vertically, laterally or both during the swing, issues can arise.

As the body efficiently coils around a stable lower base/body and weight is placed on the inside of the trail foot during the backswing, power is effortlessly developed and is ready to be just as effortlessly released on the downswing. Every successful professional on tour may have very different styles but all have the same efficiently timed body sequence. Imagine a wave of energy working from the feet, to the core, up through the arms and into the club.

To appreciate the principle of 'working from the ground upwards' picture doing a vertical jump in the air. The power begins from a big surge from the lower body, and energy is transferred up through the body and out through the tips of the hands. If you were to reverse that movement and create power from the upper body to jump high, very little energy would be produced.

This principle of working from the ground upwards applies in exactly the same way in reference to the golf swing. If an attempt to create distance is generated from the upper body alone, power, efficiency and certainly accuracy are greatly lost. Utilising the ground with a stable lower base is crucial, not only in rotating the body during the backswing, but also unwinding into the downswing and impact. Anytime the sequence of lower body/pelvis, thorax, arms and club are mismatched in any way during the transition into the downswing, power and accuracy are potentially compromised.

Another way golfers may try to create power to gain more distance is through excessive thrusting of the hips forwards and upwards at impact. This, however, leaves the club trailing behind the body and in turn (amongst other issues) creates less pressure on the ball. This can often happen when trying to swing faster and hit the ball harder. The golf swing is a combination of the hands, arms and body, if they become out of sync, power and accuracy are lost. Yes, the body must continue to turn through the shot, (Imagine the swinging chairs at the amusement park, the centre of the carousel must continue moving to ensure the chairs on the outside continue to move in an orderly fashion), however the arms must have a chance to catch up.

Develop the sensation of an efficient body motion with drills and exercises

Using body drills without a golf club can help to gain the feeling of an efficient body motion. World leading tour coach, Pete Cowen, created a drill aptly named 'The Spiral Staircase' which promotes an efficient body motion whilst utilising ground forces. Here is how it works.

Create your normal posture position, cross your arms over your chest or alternatively place a club behind your shoulders. From here rotate your torso into the backswing, feeling the weight starting to work through the trail foot. For a right handed golfer, transfer weight from the left foot into the right ankle, left ankle into the right shin, left shin into the right knee, left knee into the right thigh, left thigh into the right hip and so on. Create the sensation of winding the body against its closest ally, the ground. Almost imagine the body as a corkscrew, working from the ground upwards. Eliminate any lifting of the spine, tilting or sliding to the side. A mirror can be used to assist. From here, transition into the downswing, with the sensation of a **small** squat as you transfer weight from the right foot into the left ankle, right ankle into the left shin, right shin into the left knee and so as the body turns through the shot. Again no sliding or excessive lifting is necessary, simply an unwinding of the body whilst utilising the ground forces. If you were to do the exercise against a wall, imagine your tail bone maintaining relatively the same distance from the wall throughout the swing until the ball has been struck. Turn through and complete to the follow through.

At times physical limitations may restrict the ability for this motion to happen naturally; hence, as mentioned earlier, compensations can creep in. This is where physical screenings and golf specific fitness professionals can assist to establish if there are any stability or mobility issues. If so, a programme of exercises may be suggested or alternatively a slightly less dynamic movement may be an option to work around any limitations found. There are times where it can simply be a motor learning skill that needs developing and there are exercises for this to help develop the correct feeling. Physically, the gluteal muscles and core abdominal muscles play a key role in stabilising the body not only during the posture but also throughout the swing, both during the backswing and downswing. The greater the stability of the lower body combined with mobility of the hips and upper body, the greater chance of achieving distance without excessive force. This is also where a golf specific training programme can very much reap its rewards. Ref www.mytpi.com

Men are from Mars women are from Venus!

A common question often asked over the years is if dramatic differences lie between male and female golfers from a technical coaching perspective. In answer to this I have generally found that a slight pattern has evolved in how each attempt to gain extra power and distance, and how they approach it in a slightly different way based on how men and women are built differently. Due to the physiological differences, we do at times try to seek out those extra yards in different ways. Of course every individual is just that – an individual, and it doesn't necessarily apply across the board in every situation. There are female body builders and petite gentlemen all across the world who find their own ways of hitting the golf ball! However as a general rule of the thumb, in my experience there are a few patterns that appear due to the differences in physiology.

Physiological differences

Owing to the hormonal differences between men and women there are a couple of key physiological comparisons that can place an impact on how the golf club is swung. Testosterone and oestrogen play major roles when it comes to muscle size and flexibility. Testosterone, which naturally shows itself in greater quantities in men, increases everything from the size and mass of muscles to the male skeleton. Oestrogen, which shows itself in greater quantities in women, means women's bodies are potentially less muscular, but joints are more flexible with a greater range of motion. In particular, oestrogen widens the hips of females adding greater muscle mobility in abdominal regions and increased hip flexibility (in preparation for pregnancy). According to the U.S. Office of Science,

> 'The male-female muscle comparison becomes particularly polarized when it comes to the upper body where muscle fibres and lean tissues are much larger in the male physique. In contrast, oestrogen widens the hips of females adding greater muscle mobility in abdominal regions'.

> 'When it comes to hip action females dominate the range of motion scene at all ages. Increased hip flexibility is a by-product of female hormones that for millennia have been working their magic to prepare women for pregnancy'. *Nancy Reese et al; 2002, 'Joint range of motion and muscle length testing'*

So what impact does this have on the golf swing? With the above in mind, owing to the overall flexibility, and particularly in the pelvis and hip region, when striving for distance, the female golfer can have a greater tendency to create excessive body motion both rotationally and vertically during the backswing. A good range of motion can certainly be a positive, and of course it is important to have mobility in the hips, however if overdone and where it is not combined with stability, power and consistency can be compromised. As mentioned previously, the golf swing works from the ground upwards, where the lower body acts as a relatively stable base. In the case of excessive mobility without stabilisation, where the upper and lower body turn in equal amounts during the backswing (hips and shoulders), resistance, power and consistency are reduced.

Strengthening the core abdominal muscle area and the gluteal muscles would greatly assist in stabilising the body, both dynamically during the swing, and also statically within the set up and posture, generating a more stable and efficient power house. This of course does apply to both male and female golfers however due to the greater mobility within the hip region within ladies this can certainly be advantageous. Pilates can provide a fantastic option to develop core/gluteal strength and stability. This can also be beneficial where injury prevention is concerned.

Stabilisation of the upper body can also be an issue for female golfers. Studies at the department of sports medicine at Ohio State University Wexner Medical Centre, show through magnetic resonance imaging (MRI) that women have about 40 percent less upper-body mass than men do. This means that *in general*, a woman's natural upper body is only about 50 to 60 percent as strong as a man's. As mentioned previously, we must remember that every individual is different and there are some women who do not fit into this generalisation. With this in mind, increasing upper body strength in order to stabilise and support the golf club during the backswing, would be an advantage. Simple exercises supporting one's own body weight can be sufficient to make a significant impact without the need for heavy weights at the gym! A great positive is that relying on timing and rhythm versus sheer muscle power and strength can in fact also be beneficial as it can enable a greater amount of pressure to be applied to the ball at impact, along with the potential of a more centred hit, both ultimately producing a greater chance of improved distance.

Developing wrist and forearm strength can also assist female golfers with supporting the correct hand/wrist action and the golf club during the backswing. (Simply squeezing a squash ball repetitively or a similar alternative is a great exercise).

As a comparison, gents tend to be a little tighter in the hip and pelvis area. The upper body is generally a little stronger and with greater bulk. (Stability and strength are great attributes; the only downside is if mobility is compromised) This can have the potential to create a more upper body dominant motion, particularly when striving for extra yardage. The swing can get a little on the short side due to any potential limitation in mobility or alternatively the body will find another cheating mechanism to find its way into the backswing. There can also tend to be the inclination to use the dominance and power of the upper body to lead the transitional movement into the downswing.

Increasing the range of motion and flexibility within these areas, opening up both the hip and upper body (shoulder/chest) areas could help improve overall mobility, relying less on muscular, and often, tension filled bulk.

To stress once again, these are generalisations and simply observations in patterns of how male and female golfers, due to the physiological/hormonal differences, can have slightly different swing patterns when attempting to gain distance. Power and distance are not reliant on muscle bulk, excessive speed or excessive body motion, but a simple combination of stability, mobility and efficiency, allowing both men and women to maximise their strengths and get the most out of their game!

Intuitive Golf

We rely on our instincts for many things we do in everyday life, especially when generating power, accuracy and balance. At times with the golf club in our hands we have a tendency to make life a little bit harder for ourselves. Creating a simplified motion generated from a more natural starting position and a swing where natural forces are able to assist us in the process, allows for a much more repeatable movement and in turn greater consistency. Golf doesn't need to feel like hard work, the more we battle and force the club into unnatural positions the harder it is to gain success consistently and it certainly doesn't seem quite as enjoyable! When we begin to become aware of any excess tension we can begin to gain an awareness of the weight of the club head and in turn a greater awareness of where the club head is during the golf swing. With this in place it becomes easier to allow natural forces to help slot the golf club into position, it begins to assist in developing feel and also feels as though we have more control over our games and development. As mentioned previously, it is in fact letting go a little that gives us more control as oppose to feeling as though we need to guide, steer and control the golf club.

To simplify matters it may be helpful to use your everyday intuitive instincts to make golf easier for yourself. For example, think of things that you may do in everyday life that you naturally carry out without thinking about how you do them. Take the example of throwing a ball (over arm).

You take your stance, legs ample width apart; knowing that too wide will cause restrictions and too narrow a loss of stability. You naturally hold the ball more so in your fingers, knowing that grasping the ball tightly in the palm would inhibit natural hand action and make it much harder work to generate effortless power. You then let the throwing arm extend from the shoulder, rotate the body, whilst allowing the natural hand action from the wrist and fold from the elbow (In the case of the golf swing the right elbow will naturally fold during the backswing rather than the left – for a right handed golfer). If you created too much tension and purely used the arm as one lever, instincts tell you that again this will cause limitations. You also know that if you don't turn your body, power is inhibited. You anchor the weight around your right foot (right handed) knowing that excessive weight placed on your left foot or sliding to the outside of the right foot will lose power. As you start to throw towards your target, you transfer the weight to the left foot, turn the body from the ground upwards and release. You wouldn't quit or decelerate half way through, lean back or finish with your weight on your back foot or drive ahead with your upper body losing your balance. You would let the throwing arm continue to its target whilst the body naturally turned out of the way. You know intuitively where the power sources come from without having to think about it, you know that less tension is more efficient and you also know it would benefit to throw in balance.

With the golf club in our hands we sometimes forget these natural instincts and try to utilise other methods, which in turn often creates the opposite of our desired results. Where the golf swing is concerned, less is often more, simplifying matters and relying on natural forces and instincts as much as possible makes the game a great deal easier.

In summary, a great aid to achieving increased distance is to unravel any misperceptions about what creates power and distance and understand the basic principles that will enable added yardage with greater ease. Unfortunately the ways in which we try to force distance, such as turning as much as possible, swinging as fast as our body permits, gripping the club for dear life, often create the opposite of the desired effect. Sheer strength, excess or pure muscle power, will not do the trick. This is why you may see a small-framed senior golfer or petite lady boom it down the fairway yet a 6ft power house pops it just a short distance ahead. Timing and efficiency are paramount, and when both are synchronised, greater pressure and power can be employed - Powerless effort versus effortless power.

THE SHORT STUFF

'The only way to win tournaments is with the short game. Over half your shots out here are within 30 or 40 yards. Ball striking is where I'm trying to improve, yes, but more to eliminate big numbers than make birdies' – **Phil Mickleson**

I believe an improvement within the short game can make one of the biggest differences in the shortest amounts of time to any golfer. Many times as a coach, frequent requests from students come in the form of perfecting the swing or getting an extra 15/20 yards of distance. These are 'nice to haves' but ultimately when it comes down to noticing a significant improvement in your game in a short amount of time, **the short game is key.** The importance of the basic fundamentals and a well-rounded mindset discussed throughout the enclosed chapters provide strong pillars to support success not only within the long game but also within this very important element of the game.

Decide on the shot you wish to play and commit to it.

One of the biggest issues within the short game tends to arise when there are uncertainties of the intended shot ahead. When you play a short approach shot with the mind-set of just hoping to 'land it up there somewhere' without a clear intention and visual of the shot ahead it prevents you from preparing correctly and does not allow you to fully commit with confidence - and that applies to any shot in golf. Very often, if there is a poor visual image that lacks a clearly defined intention of the shot in hand, its flight or landing area, things start to become a little bit of a hit and hope scenario. With an uncertainty of whether you are trying to play a low running chip shot, medium-flighted pitch or a high soft landing lob shot, panic tends to set in. Technical issues can creep in as a result, potentially in the form of deceleration or a last minute increase in tension amongst other possible scenarios; confidence, commitment and intention to the shot at hand are diminished. Admittedly, for a beginner this will all progress in time, once the fundamentals feel a little more in place.

Practice that involves experimenting with different shots, landing areas and so forth, along with the understanding of which shot to play where will greatly increase confidence and reduce the risk of uncertainty. A clear visual and intention of the shot in hand are crucial for successful results. Decide and commit to the chosen shot, establish a clear visual of the ball flight, the landing area and the remaining roll of the ball upon landing and confirm the ideal club selection. This combined with solid foundations and dedication to time spent on the practice area, will enable you to be well on your way to saving shots around the green and improving your score. Be creative and enjoy the process.

Short game practice

Time spent practising the short game is time extremely well spent. I really can't emphasise that enough. When we spend time on this key element of the game, it allows us to experiment with the components of the set up and swing that enable the control of the ball flight and distance. It also allows us to be creative in developing the different types of short game shots. When we are on the golf course it can be tempting to go with a trusted stock shot. Even if that shot isn't necessarily the right option, it may be the only one we know or trust and hence play it all the time. Having a stock shot that we know we can rely on isn't necessarily a bad thing. However, if it prevents us from experimenting with other options that may be more beneficial, it can create limitations.

Here is an example: Let's say you really like your sand iron and you like to play a high flighted shot, one that spends most of its time in the air when you get close to the green. If the only shot you have in the bag is a lofted sand iron it can create limitations in certain situations and at times leaves little room for error. Imagine a pin position at the back of a large green, it's a windy day and you are on a golf course during the height of summer, where the fairways have become hard and fairly bare. To play that high lofted, high flighted sand iron successfully it will require a solid strike, perfectly judged distance control and a hope that the windy conditions don't grab hold of it. The heightened pressure those elements add to the shot, thrown in with any additional tension, can make it very difficult to get the ball close to the hole on a consistent basis. Now if you were confident that your stock shot got you close to the hole 9 times out of 10, fantastic, no one can argue with that or encourage you to change, however if there are inconsistencies, those are the times where it is worth experimenting with other options. If you have the options of a low, medium and high flighted shot you are in a position of greater flexibility when it comes to playing to different pin positions, different greens, distances, landing areas, lies and weather conditions.

The practice area is a great place to experiment with different pin positions, distances and types of short shots. As mentioned a little earlier, avoid spending too much time practising your favourite shot or distance. Instead, use the practice ground to step out of your comfort zone. If you like a full distance pitch but not the shorter shots that require alterations in the swing and set up, be sure to practise those; you are going to be faced with them on the course so it's better to become familiar, build confidence and experiment with them on the practice area first. One of the reasons shorter shots that require less than a full swing can sometimes feel less comfortable to practice and can at times feel less consistent is due to the fact that if there are any technical issues or if the club is out of position in some way there is less time to recover prior to impact within a shorter motion. It can at times highlight problem areas a little more. Seeking professional guidance may assist with the process.

If contact and flight are fairly consistent however, then it may simply be a case of developing feel through practice to gain confidence in altering the length of swing required for certain distances and building greater distance control. It is better to gain the feeling of shortening the overall length of the swing with a smooth positive acceleration for a shorter pitch shot than having a fuller length swing that remains similar for every approach shot and either trying to change the speed of the downswing or opting for a more lofted club each time. Using a fuller motion and attempting to control the distance primarily with the speed of the downswing in the form of deceleration will impact the quality of the contact. Simply changing the club and loft of club each time can provide some success but tends to reduce the variety of shot available for various conditions, i.e weather and pin positions. A motion that has variability in its length where required (combined with the adjustments necessary in the set up fundamentals) can improve the quality and consistency of contact and will also enable greater flexibility both in the trajectory and also how the ball responds upon landing, i.e. the amount of roll.

As mentioned previously developing scoring games that re-create more of the scenario you will find yourself in out on the course will assist in instilling greater confidence. Playing from the same spot and distance repetitively may not reap as successful rewards; yes there are certainly benefits to this form of repetitive practice in the form of consistency and developing the quality of technique and contact, but variety must ideally be blended in at some point. Practise with experimentation, variety, fun and focus to create the most significant improvements to your results.

Putting

> *'Never try to look like anyone else when you're putting, you have to be yourself when you putt.'* - Harvey Penick.

Putting is another key area of your short game where improvement will significantly lead to lower scores. As a coach a key role is to simplify the road to success and where possible find the most efficient route. Improving or reducing the amount of putts per round, I believe, is certainly one of those routes. If you compare the scenarios of two rounds played consecutively over two days. Day one is not such a good day and you end up three putting every green. Day two however is considerably better to the degree of reducing your average to two putts per green, a saving of 18 shots!

I admit that this is an extreme example, yet it is possible. Now imagine trying to improve your score by 18 shots over two days by improving your distance off the tee by 10/15 yards, a much more difficult task. However, this is the area where many amateur golfers spend a great deal of time, effort and focus. This example is purely to highlight the dramatic difference an improvement in your putting skills can make on your score and handicap in a relatively short space of time and to help generate a picture of how your focus may be spent in a more productive and effective way.

Putting does not want to be seen as an overly technical or mechanical part of the game. It relies heavily on feel, trust, imagination, visualisation and green-reading abilities. It is for this reason that the putting green is the one area where you will see quite a wide variety of styles amongst the professional ranks. The underlying core fundamentals amongst good putters, however, will still generally remain very similar. The emphasis for the purpose of this chapter will be based around developing a routine, trust and feel.

Developing a pre-shot putting routine

> *A routine is not a routine if you have to think about it' – Davis Love Jnr*

How many times have you frustratingly missed that short six inch tap in whilst hastily trying to finish the hole after you have missed that initial first or second putt?! You only have to look at the best players in the world to notice the care and attention taken over each and every putt. No matter what the length or the consequences, they have some form of routine over every putt. I have often found that the feedback received about a putting routine is the worry that it takes too long to do over every putt and that playing partners may be held up by slow play. I understand that this could be a concern however the few extra seconds it takes to carry out a short routine can easily be made up either elsewhere on the course or in fewer putts, and can be absolutely priceless in return.

So what would the routine contain? As with all pre-shot routines, they are personal to each individual. The actual breakdown of what the routine contains can vary from person to person. Most importantly when putting, it is the opportunity to:

    Gain a sense of the speed and distance of the putt

    Assess the contours of the green

    Create a clear visual of the intended line

    Have a moment to gain a sense of calm and relaxed focus

The latter point in itself can be one of the most beneficial elements to creating a consistent pre-shot putting routine. The minute panic sets in and we try to get the job over with as quickly as possible we begin to enter a downward spiral of missed putts, frustration, a drop in confidence and a few extra shots on the scorecard. Experiment with creating a putting routine, it doesn't have to be a long-winded affair, but allow yourself the opportunity of those priceless few extra seconds of care and focus on the greens.

Don't forget to breathe!!

The importance of correct breathing is discussed in other areas of the book; however in relation to putting it can play a significant role. For some golfers, breathing and putting, would you believe, don't always go hand in hand, particularly when the stakes are high! I have witnessed many times where students have in fact held their breath tightly until the putt is over or have simply forgotten to breathe! If we hold our breath with excessive tension during the set up or through the impact area of a putt or both combined, it reduces the ability of a relaxed stroke. So what problems arise from this? Firstly, putting very much relies on feel; distance control becomes much easier when you have a degree of relaxation and in turn greater feel. U.S Open winner, Ben Crenshaw, states that the only tension he feels in the putting stroke is a light pressure in his finger tips. Crenshaw said,

> 'It allows you to feel the weight of the putter head much more'.

Additionally, when you excessively hold your breath through impact, the strike can become much more of an aggressive hit, rather than a smooth positive acceleration. This encourages an inconsistent roll on the ball. The ball will either fire off the putter face too quickly, causing too much pace, or will skid off the putter face causing an inconsistent roll and potentially slower pace. On the flip side it can also be the case where a deceleration through impact can arise. Generating a feeling of exhaling through impact can help to create a smooth and consistent positive acceleration, allowing for a more consistent roll and pace. Combine this with a stable centre and head position throughout the stroke and it creates a much smoother pendulum motion and in turn greater consistency of pace and accuracy.

Experiment with a few balls a couple of feet from the hole on the practice putting green. Simply breathe in on the backstroke and exhale on the through stroke. It will at the very least give you a feeling of the comparison, both in the strike and a relaxed, smooth, yet positive acceleration through impact. You should start to find a positive and consistent roll on the ball and a string of successfully holed putts!

I really can't emphasise enough how beneficial it is to put that extra bit of time, care and attention into developing your short game, and the positive effect it will have on your game and results. This applies to all abilities. Simply gaining a level of consistency that provides the security of knowing that once you approach the greens you have it reasonably well-covered will pay dividends. Replacing any destruction within your short game with consistency puts far greater ease on the remainder of your game and instils a level of confidence that no matter what, from a scoring point of view, you are going to be, as they say 'In the ball park!' Whether it means converting a par into a birdie or preventing several dropped shots, beneficial gains can be made with a little extra care, time and focus on this vital area of the game.

THE MID ROUND SLUMP

'When health is absent, wisdom cannot reveal itself, art cannot manifest, strength cannot fight, wealth becomes useless and intelligence cannot be applied' - Herophilus

A commonly used term to describe a drop in performance during a round is the 'mid round slump'. Generally, this may happen anywhere between holes twelve to seventeen. Up to this point, things have been going well until all of a sudden, it feels as though the wheels have come off and the harder you try the worse it gets. A big contributing factor to this, which often goes unnoticed, is a lack of hydration and nutritional energy.

The importance of nutrition and hydration in golf

The importance of a healthy and balanced nutritional intake can be likened to that of a finely tuned sports car. Imagine driving a Ferrari with little or no fuel or even low grade fuel for that matter, it's not going to go too far and certainly cannot function at its maximum capacity. The human body is no exception and in this context, neither is the golfer. The best golf swing in the world will not achieve its maximum potential if the body is undernourished or dehydrated. The human body gets its fuel from the nutrients contained in food and drink. A variety of these nutrients are needed to keep fit and healthy particularly if you are generally active, take part in sport or set individual challenges. The nutrients in our food provide energy, promote growth and development, and regulate our bodily functions. Our body depends on these nutrients, as it is unable to produce sufficient amounts on its own. As golf is not necessarily seen in the same category as other more physically enduring sporting activities, the impact of nutrition and hydration on golfing performance can often get a little neglected.

Let's take the all too common scenario where you have a mid-morning tee time. Perhaps you get way laid first thing, which means you have a last minute dash out of the house to get to the golf club on time. You pull up into the car park, grab a quick takeaway coffee and rush on to the first tee without any time for breakfast. After 9 holes you are starting to feel a little weary, thirsty, and think maybe it's time for some sustenance. On the 10th tee you search through your golf bag and, alas, all you can find is a can of soft drink and a chocolate bar from two weeks last Tuesday!

So what could be the golfing consequences of this sequence of events? The word 'breakfast' comes from the fact that you are literally 'breaking the fast' from the hours of rest and repair, which your body has been making during the night. Your body is also at its most dehydrated state when you first wake up in the morning. Having been in too much of a rush to prepare anything, your body is now in a deficient state of vital nutrients and hydration. The chocolate bar may provide an initial boost in energy but following the peak, an extreme drop may occur. The soft drink contains high levels of sugar and potentially caffeine (depending on the variety) but unfortunately very little hydrating qualities. To an already dehydrated body (on top of the coffee drunk earlier), the extra caffeine rush from, let's say cola as being the soft drink of choice, provides little nutritional content other than to potentially raise the heart rate and cause another peak and trough in energy. To some, this may seem like an extreme example, to others it may sound a little on the familiar side! Regardless, under these circumstances it becomes much harder to perform at your optimal. To summarise this scenario any depletion prior to the round and during the first half of the round which is then fixed with sweet unhealthy foods can potentially cause further blood glucose fluctuations over the following few hours and even within the remainder of the round. It becomes a little clearer to see where those mid-round slumps of fatigue, loss of concentration and poor on-course decisions may stem from.

'To keep the body in good health is a duty...otherwise we shall not be able to keep our mind strong and clear' - Buddha

The importance of hydration

Firstly we will address the importance of correct hydration and the implications if left neglected. 18 holes of golf require a relatively high level of concentration and a degree of physical stamina to achieve successful results. Maintaining the body's hydration levels will certainly assist in this process. Any form of dehydration may create a variety of symptoms of which include; headache, light-headedness, fatigue and nausea meaning physical activity becomes more difficult and performance drops. Mental function is also reduced, which can have negative implications for decision-making, concentration and motor control, all of which may greatly affect scoring capabilities, course management skills and overall performance on the golf course.

To eliminate any of these symptoms monitor your levels of hydration and take precautions before problems arise. You can monitor your level of hydration in different ways. Monitoring urine colour and frequency provides a good gauge to work from. Frequent passing of pale coloured urine is a sign of good hydration. Remember, dehydration is cumulative, so you can become dehydrated over a number of days. As in other sports it is important not to wait until you are thirsty, in golf it is particularly important as a drop in concentration levels is one of the first symptoms of dehydration. When you reach a point of feeling thirsty, the body is already dehydrated. Water is continually being eliminated through our breath, sweat and urine and therefore, must be replaced every day by consuming appropriate food and fluids. After oxygen, water is a close second on the list of the essential nutrients for life and it makes up 50-75% of an adults body weight. Exact needs depend on a number of elements, including weather conditions and levels of physical activity.

On average we should ideally **drink a minimum of one and a half litres of water every day**. With warmer climates and increased physical exertion this amount will increase. On the golf course, the key is to **not** wait until you are thirsty and then consume large amounts in one go. Take a few sips every two or three holes, do not wait until you reach the 10th tee or later.

In warmer climates the vitamin, mineral and electrolyte content of sports/fitness waters may also aid performance and be a little more palatable than plain water. The inclusion of flavourings and sodium may help to increase the fluid intake and the inclusion of sodium may also aid fluid absorption and retention. They also have fewer calories than highly concentrated sports drinks and are easier to consume. Some of the sports drinks available can contain a high volume of sugar providing unnecessary calories leading to potential weight gain with regular use and little nutritional gain for the task at hand, in this instance, golf. There are 3 categories of sports drinks on the market - Isotonic, hypotonic and hypertonic. In simple terms the carbohydrate and electrolyte content will be either the same, more dilute or more concentrated than the body fluids. This determines the speed at which the fluid will be absorbed by the body. Each option will provide different benefits, the greater carbohydrate content the more energy will be provided, the lower the carbohydrate content, the greater hydration.

Hypotonic drinks - Contain fluid, electrolytes and a low level of carbohydrate (less than 4g per 100ml) For this reason it provides rapid fluid replacement.

Isotonic drinks - Quickly replaces fluids lost by sweating and supplies a boost of carbohydrate. Most commercial isotonic drinks contain 4-8g carbohydrate per 100ml

Hypertonic drinks - Contain a high level of carbohydrate. The primary focus is on energy supplies versus rehydration. Often used by ultra distance athletes to meet energy demands.

Alcohol, black tea, coffee, caffeinated energy drinks, highly concentrated fruit juices and fizzy soft drinks are to be avoided where possible as they can act as diuretics (encouraging fluid loss), may be high in sugar, create an increase in heart rate and affect concentration levels. They are ideally not to be used as substitutes for water or fitness water/diluted squash.

The importance of nutrition

The food we eat also plays a key role in sustaining energy levels. Once again the key is balance and moderation, as alluded to previously extreme highs and lows of energy can negatively affect performance. Try not to wait until you begin to feel tired and hungry, eat the correct nutrients little and often to sustain constant and balanced energy levels.

Nutritionally there are a few key guidelines that may help you to avoid those slumps and give you the best possible chance of maximising your potential throughout the full 18 holes of your round and avoiding the mid-round slump:

- Carry healthy snacks in your golf bag which ideally combine complex carbohydrates, protein and healthy fats – cereal bars, dried fruit, nuts, bananas, wholemeal sandwiches with healthy fat/ protein filling, e.g. chicken/almond butter.

- Eat little and often ensuring energy levels are kept constant rather than extreme highs and lows.

- Eat a balanced diet combining the required fruits, vegetables, protein, carbohydrates and healthy fats.

- Prepare meals and snacks in advance rather than leaving it to chance and grabbing any available food on the day.

- If playing in the morning get up that little bit earlier to ensure you have a carbohydrate and protein rich breakfast e.g. Scrambled egg on wholemeal toast, wholemeal bagel with almond butter. Avoid fried food or food high in saturated fat that may lay a little heavier on the stomach or be a little harder to digest.

More detailed dietary guidelines are widely available which specialise in various areas whether that be for weight loss, endurance sports or allergies, as examples. The key aim here is simply to highlight the fact that any deficiencies within the areas of nutrition and hydration can have a key impact on performance for **all** levels of golfer.

This area can get a little neglected amongst many amateur golfers, potentially feeling that the principles only apply or make a difference to the elite or professionals within the game. The professionals are in fact great ones to mimic; they understand the importance it has on their performance. You will often find them snacking on a banana or sipping water every couple of holes. Adopting a healthy approach and awareness to your fluid intake and eating habits will not only allow you to maximise your potential on the golf course but also allow you to lead a healthier lifestyle and greater sense of well-being away from it. A win win all round! Give yourself the opportunity to perform at your best, your mind, body and game will thank you for it!

WHY ISN'T THIS POSITIVE THINKING WORKING?!

'Nothing binds you except your thoughts. Nothing limits you except your fears. And nothing controls you except your beliefs' – *Marianne Williamson*

The modern golfing era is increasingly moving away from basing itself purely around technique and greater importance is being placed not only on the overall well being of the individual but specifically on the mental and emotional side of the game. The importance of performance mind-set has become increasingly apparent within all walks of sporting life. There are some fantastic books available providing information on how to master the mental side of sport in general, and golf in particular. I read many of these books whilst I was struggling with any form of consistency and success during my competitive years as a golfer. I found that I had a good understanding of how to think properly and what I **should** be thinking, but unfortunately it didn't seem to produce the desired results. This is certainly not to blame the quality of the information in any way. But on reflection, I believe there were a couple of key reasons my approach in **trying** to create a successful, confident and positive mind-set on the golf course didn't seem to work. There were times when I had read so much about what I should be thinking that in the end on the golf course my mind was filled with thinking about what I should be thinking about!

The key with changing old habits of thought, or creating and allowing a more positive and fruitful mind-set, is that in just the same way we work on a new movement on the driving range with repetition, or we go to the gym to build our muscles, **exactly the same principle applies to our mindset.** Creating change happens not just on the golf course, but away from it too. If we only try to think positively during those first three, nine or even eighteen holes on the golf course, then decide it's not working, give ourselves a hard time, convince ourselves that we can't even think positively, get frustrated and give up on it, the results will not be the fruitful ones we were hoping for.

We have to be gentle with ourselves and also endeavour to adopt the principles of a supportive and positive mind-set aside from the golf course. How we talk to ourselves for the remainder of the 24-hour clock, away from the golf course, is very often going to tie in with how we talk to ourselves on it. If we give ourselves a hard time in everyday life its very unlikely we will transform into a forgiving, compassionate and optimistic golfer when on the course, my guess is there will be no letting ourselves off the hook there either! This is where our work begins, not just when we have a golf club in our hands. Awareness of our mindset during the remaining hours before and after our rounds will enable the opportunity for consistent change.

I often found myself with an internal battle on the golf course. Having read and acknowledged the concepts of 'positive thinking' I would try and hammer away at the negative thoughts and try to force positive ones in their place, whilst at the same time, feeling annoyed at myself for even thinking those negative thoughts in the first place. After all, I should at least know how to think positively after having read what felt like the whole encyclopaedia on sports psychology! As you can imagine, tension is increasing by the minute in this scenario with little room for a free flowing golf swing or an enjoyable day on the golf course. A quiet mind will serve you far greater than an internal battle of trying to think the most positive thought possible. If you find yourself on the golf course with an internal battle of 'trying to think positively' simply acknowledging any negative thought that is not serving you and incrementally adjusting it or letting it go completely will provide greater benefit and help to ease any resistance and tension.

Embracing a positive thought process and mindset, one which becomes a lifestyle choice, rather than a forced process when you are on the course will offer greater success and reduce frustrations.

Ideally, it becomes a part of everyday life rather than thinking about how you should be thinking during your round of golf! Building awareness around and encouraging a healthy mindset through every area of your life will not only become your default programme on the golf course producing more positive results, but also generate the potential for greater well-being off the course. Imagine the night before an important round of golf. You are lying in bed replaying all of the potential nightmare scenarios that may happen the next day, going out of bounds on the first hole or even, heaven forbid, finishing last in the tournament! You tee up the next day and think, right, I'm going to think positively today! You already begin to feel a slight internal battle as if you are kidding yourself in some way. Why isn't this positive thinking enough? Unfortunately in this scenario quite a lot of negative momentum of uncertainty and doubt has already been built. How we feel and how we talk to ourselves outside of the golf course has an impact. Therefore, if we try to layer that with a dose of positive thinking purely on the day of a particular round, it may become a frustrating rollercoaster of inconsistency.

Another reason why I believe 'positive thinking' doesn't always work out the way people foresee is due to the deep seated, often unconscious thought patterns and beliefs that lie below the surface of people's consciousness. Let me explain a little about the conscious and subconscious parts of the mind.

The conscious and subconscious mind

The conscious mind is the creative, analytical, logical and decision-making part of our brain. It also forms a person's wishes and desires, and is held in what is known as the pre-frontal cortex in the brain. In context to the golf course and our game, it is the part of the brain that decides what club to take, the wind direction and what handicap we wish to aspire to. Research tells us that we operate from the conscious mind approximately 5% of the time during the day.

The subconscious mind is where we hold our memories, beliefs and emotions. It acts as a large tape recorder. You can also imagine it as the hard drive in your computer. The subconscious mind is also responsible for the functions carried out daily throughout our bodies (via the Autonomic Nervous System). If you were to consciously think about having to pump the 200 gallons of blood around your body every hour at the same time as regulating all of the body's other moment by moment functions, things could get a bit tricky! The subconscious mind processes information much faster than the conscious mind. The subconscious mind is also non-judgemental to the information it receives, it simply stores the information programmed into it. Psychologists have often likened the differences between the two in the form of an iceberg. The conscious mind is the tip of the iceberg and the remainder below the surface is the subconscious mind.

Imagine sitting on top of the iceberg with your positive thoughts and desires heading in one direction. In golfing terms it may be the goal of reducing your handicap, for example. Below the surface, where the bulk of the iceberg lies, are your beliefs, memories and emotions. If they are working in opposition to your goals and desires and are moving in the other direction, the goals will feel at times, like a perpetual uphill struggle. However, when the two are in alignment, conscious and subconscious mind in tandem, and beliefs, emotions and desires are all working in the same direction, limitless possibilities of human potential arise.

> *'We operate from the conscious mind less than 5% of the day. Unless the subconscious mind has the same programming as the conscious mind, the power of positive thinking will not work'* – Dr Bruce Lipton

Often when we 'try' to think or verbalise positive statements, they are coming from the conscious mind. If underlying subconscious beliefs and emotions do not correspond with the conscious thought, ones which have potentially become a programmed pattern of habit, the positive statement will be less effective. If there is a large emotional gap between what we desire and what we believe, there is greater resistance and tension. When you really want something but you believe in its opposition, there is a strong tug of war inside you.

Subconscious beliefs held below the surface, at times unnoticed, have often been programmed or learned by us from a young age. Up until the age of seven, the brain operates in a slower brain wave frequency called theta waves, the same frequency used in hypnosis, which is why young babies and children frequently appear as if they are in a trance like state. In this theta frequency the brain is in a very programmable state, a bit like a sponge. This means that it is open to new things. It is at this point that we take on board the thoughts, beliefs and opinions of those around us, namely parents. If these programmes are positive, this is fantastic and will serve us well. If not, unfortunately they can stay with us into our adult life and show themselves in self-sabotaging ways, tripping us up on our way to our desires and wishes.

Research suggests that 70% of our subconscious programmes or learned behaviour is negative and self-sabotaging. Above the age of seven, our brain frequency increases to what is known as alpha waves, and from around 14 years of age onwards it increases yet again to beta waves, which is the everyday alert waking state. On the other end of the spectrum are Delta waves, which occur in the deep state of sleep. Whilst we are trying to consciously (and potentially sporadically) think these positive thoughts out on the golf course, we may have subconscious programmes and beliefs running. As an example, we may have the belief that we are not good enough or worthy of achieving our goals. If this subconsciously learned programme has built up so much momentum over time and is the default it can override the desire or 'positive thinking'. Think of the athlete who trips at the final hurdle or that tee shot you fire out of bounds on the last hole!

'We create success or failure on the course, primarily by our thoughts' – Gary Player

Changing our programmes

The word 'programme' in this context refers to our repetitive thoughts and language and how they affect our actions and behaviour. I believe the first step to changing negative programmes lies in gaining awareness and an understanding as to why our best intentions and positive thinking haven't quite been getting the results we were after. How any negative programmes and deep seated beliefs have been thwarting our best efforts. Once we acknowledge this we can then at least become easier on ourselves knowing that we haven't failed at this 'positive thinking' which as a starting point, will begin to release built-up frustrations and tension. This then creates a far better platform to move forward from and one from which we can begin to make positive changes.

The following chapters will go a little more into the area of beliefs and limiting beliefs. However, to change our learned negative programmes, a few key aspects will make this easier to achieve.

Firstly, as mentioned above, an awareness of the negative programme/belief is vital, without this, positive change becomes an uphill struggle, feeling as though it's a one step forward two steps back process. We now know that a deep seated belief may not be glaringly obvious, this is where a little internal reflection or even help from a trained therapist may assist. Golf seems to provide a great platform to discover any hindering negative beliefs we have about ourselves. Many other sports encourage us to utilise our natural instincts whilst reacting to a moving ball, golf, however is based around a stationary ball. We have those few seconds prior to playing the shot which can potentially leave us wide open to any negative subconscious beliefs surfacing and sabotaging our desired outcome. It is for this reason I believe that golf can become a fantastic learning curve and a game that provides the opportunity of turning any negative frustrations into a positive journey of self discovery.

Once we have the awareness of any negative programme/belief we may have we can begin to change the hold it may have on us. We can begin to question its truth and affirm a more positive replacement. Ultimately a belief is just a thought we keep thinking.

How can we do this?

Present moment awareness, also commonly known as mindfulness keeps the conscious mind present. If the conscious mind is thinking of something ahead in the future or something in the past, the subconscious mind is running the show, any old unwanted negative programmes then take precedence, almost running as a default, automatic pilot setting. (Techniques to assist in this process can be found in chapter 19). Research into some of the practices of the Buddhist Zen Monks showed that they interestingly have a chime or bell which goes off every 15 minutes throughout the Monastery during each day; this signals and reminds them to bring their mind and focus back to the present moment. It is surprising how, without realising it, our minds often drift back to thoughts of the past or ahead into a future based focus, particularly on the golf course!

Repetition also plays a key role. Think about when you first learnt to walk. You stumbled, got back up, stumbled a few more times, and eventually you could walk without having to think about it. The program was installed. Imagine what a pain it would be if each day you woke up and you had to re learn how to walk again. The repetition of the learned program ensures it sticks.

This is one of the reasons certain negative thoughts and unwanted programs can become difficult to change. With awareness, repetition of a new affirmation and greater focus on what is wanted, combined with tending to the way you feel, a new and improved program, belief system and thought process can be installed. Imagine as a right handed person learning to write with the left hand. Initially it feels awkward and requires consistent repetition. Through consistent repetition it becomes more natural and can eventually become more instinctive. A clear intention combined with a heightened emotion begins to shift the mind and body out of the old program.

A relaxed state also assists in the process of accessing new, more positive thought patterns and beliefs. If we think back to the brain wave state of when the very first programs were installed from birth, the slower, hypnotic state of theta waves, we know that this could be the quickest and easiest way to reprogram our beliefs, ensuring they are in alignment with our desires. Often the point at which we are just about to drop off to sleep is when we begin to access this theta brain wave zone. This can become an ideal point at which we can install supporting, nourishing beliefs, thoughts and programs that align with our wishes and desires both on and off the golf course. In the morning as we awaken we are shifting from delta brainwaves of deep sleep into theta and gradually into low beta, again this can be a good time to create momentum in the direction of our desires. Without conscious awareness it is surprising how quickly our default programmes and thought patterns can sneak in! Our memorised thoughts, feelings, behaviours and actions run like an automated programme until we make a shift and become conscious. At times the simple awareness of whether the thought feels lighter or heavier puts us back in the driving seat.

Meditation also provides this relaxed state. (Meditation/mindfulness techniques will follow in later chapters) It allows a clearing of the mind, or to use an analogy - the clearing of a muddy pond. This provides a chance to release the old programmes that do not serve us. From this state resistance can be released creating a platform to enable new and more beneficial programmes, desires and beliefs to be installed. Imagine trying to upload a new programme on a computer that is already full with other programmes, it would take a long time to download and run a lot less efficiently. The obvious answer would be to remove the programmes that no longer serve the computer or user and make space for the new and more beneficial programmes. The mind is exactly the same. The beauty of this is that the choice of which beliefs and programmes are installed is always just that, a choice, we don't have to stick with anything that doesn't feel good or positively serve us.

So how do we know which programmes serve us, and which do not? The results, circumstances and environment around us pretty much reflect back to us our habitual thought patterns, programmes and beliefs. If everything around us reflects back to us exactly what we want and wish for, our thoughts, beliefs and desires are in alignment. If not, it simply highlights an opportunity for positive change and provides a platform from which to create new and improved belief systems. There is another gauge and inbuilt mechanism which helps us know if we are on or off track - Our emotions.......

THE EMOTIONAL SCALE

'What separates great players from the good ones is not so much ability as brain power and emotional equilibrium' – Arnold Palmer

Our emotions play a huge role in gauging how we are doing and what track we are on. Our in built emotional guidance system, made up of our emotions and feelings, is pivotal in any field of sporting performance. It lets us know where we are placing our focus and whether we are moving towards our desires and intentions or moving further away. It is a bit like our own internal compass. If we close ourselves off from it we lose one of our greatest companions to achieving success both in sport and in life. Think of the GPS navigation system in your car. You program in your chosen destination, it provides the quickest route and subsequently it tells you when you have missed the exit or taken a wrong turn. In choosing to ignore its guidance, you decide to turn the volume down in order to keep driving as it starts to irritate you, yet it keeps getting louder and louder the more off track you get. 'Please turn around where possible!' Your own internal GPS plays exactly the same role in the form of emotions. Using this analogy highlights the times we tend to ignore and sometimes even become numb to its guidance.

What is the emotional guidance scale?

If you have a desire or goal and you have contradictory thoughts and beliefs about achieving that goal it will manifest itself in the form of tension or resistance and create a block in achieving a successful outcome. Negative emotion is your inner guidance system prompting you that there is discordance and also highlighting when a thought isn't in alignment with your true self and potential, it becomes a red flag to change course. Ignoring this would be a bit like putting a smiley sticker over an empty petrol gauge on the dashboard of a car or turning the volume down on that GPS system mentioned earlier. Imagine two ends of a stick, on one end of the stick is what is wanted or our desire, on the other end of the stick is the lack of it or what we don't want, our emotions tell us which end of the stick we are placing greater focus.

Having previously detailed a few key concepts as to why purely trying to 'think positively' may not have always produced the results that we have wanted in the past, it would be a fair assumption to think that it is better than being all doom and gloom. The only issue lies when there is the emotional discordance between what you think, feel and believe. It is this gap that causes the tension, and added to this is the frustration and blame we put on ourselves that the 'positive thinking' isn't working! There is the opportunity to bridge that gap on a moment-by-moment basis, in turn getting you closer to the results you are after and that lies in ensuring the underlying feeling is in alignment with the corresponding thought. In other words does this thought sit, or feel right, does it feel good, or is there a niggling discordance sitting beneath the surface? If there is any discordance or resistance between what we think and what we feel we can begin making gradual emotional shifts by choosing a thought that simply allows you to feel incrementally a little better each time. This will begin to release resistance and create a feeling of relief. It is not necessary to jump from the depths of despair to the most positive emotion or thought imaginable or to a belief that at the time feels too far beyond what we feel we are able to comfortably resonate with. If we try to jump straight to feelings on the opposite end of the scale we may find a great deal of resistance, give up and simply go back to our old habits of thought.

> *'Performance can never be of a higher or lower calibre than our Emotional Energy, our attitude and mood. The often ignored intuitive wisdom of the body simply does not lie.'* – **Tim Kramer**

Here is an example in a golfing context: If you jumped from 'I never putt well' to 'I am a great putter' there is likely to be an underlying unconscious and incongruent niggling feeling of tension and disbelief. It is simply too great a jump to make in one go. You can generally gauge the emotions that accompany the statement as to whether it feels in alignment with your thoughts or 'true to you'. A misaligned feeling and thought will generally bring with it a degree of unease, there is an emotional gap. If you have been repeatedly and over time thinking a thought, such as, 'I never putt well' after a period of time it has generated momentum. This momentum begins to also create an expectation, this expectation is then fulfilled with the physical evidence of not putting well and so the cycle continues. If we try to change things immediately to 'I am a great putter' there is too much momentum favouring the old negative statement. Imagine a train travelling at 85 miles an hour in one direction and then trying to immediately go in the opposite direction at the same speed, its contents would get dislodged. This is what happens when you try to jump to an emotion that is the extreme opposite to the old and often familiar pattern. If we have a new mission to try and 'think positively' it can at times, feel uncomfortable and we are left disappointed. The key is to remember those old negative feelings are just that, they are old, yet familiar, patterns of habit. They are only your perceived reality. There is an alternative which lies in gaining conscious awareness and choosing to think a thought that **feels a little better**. A positive shift in emotion is the green light that you are moving closer to your desires and goals.

As we begin to become conscious of the language we use and utilise our inner emotional guidance system we are able to feel our way gradually and incrementally to a better feeling thought. Sounds simple, and may not seem like rocket science, however, often we become so used to repeating a negative statement about our golf or feeling a certain negative emotion that we don't even realise we are doing it or the consequences it carries. How many times have you said to yourself or out loud things such as, 'I always start the round well and finish poorly' or 'I never play well under pressure' without being aware how frequently and habitually you repeat it. Awareness brings with it the opportunity for change. Once we have the conscious awareness we can begin to change the unconscious habits of negative dialogue, which when repeated over and over, become beliefs. Remember, a belief is just a thought you keep thinking!

Once we begin to consciously change the language and thought processes, there is a change of emotion, and from there, beliefs can then also begin to change. The emotion really is the key factor, however an awareness of the language can kick start the change. A simple change in the words we use can be paramount. Changing 'I **never** putt well' to 'I **could** putt well' evokes very different emotions, simply by changing one word in the sentence. It implies a sense of hopefulness and optimism and there is a degree of belief. 'I never putt well' almost slams the door on the chance of a positive outcome and evokes very different emotions. At the same time, jumping to the other extreme of 'I am a great putter' would also generate some resistance as there is an air of disbelief.

As you begin to change your thoughts and the language you use you can begin to incrementally feel the difference in your emotions. This begins an emotional shift within you. If you make a positive statement combined with a positive emotion, results will appear. If you make a positive statement with underlying negative emotions or disbelief it will create resistance and effort, shining a bigger spot light on the exact thing that you don't want or feel in lack of! Imagine convincing yourself you are wealthy when deep down you feel and believe you are poor, maybe due to earlier programmes installed from elders around you in your younger years. Your deep seated belief and feelings will be the underlying determining factor and you end up feeling worse as it is emphasising the lack you feel in your current situation whilst you compare it to what you really want. In this instance you would either change the subject completely which would release any resistance or incrementally evoke thoughts that feel more congruent, that feel a little better, i.e. 'There are many people in my position who have moved forward to great success and wealth.' This creates a feeling of hope rather than resistance or shining a spotlight on any lack.

The Emotional Scale

Esther and Jerry Hicks, in their book 'The Astonishing Power of Emotions': Let your feelings be your guide', talk about the emotional guidance scale. Our feelings function as a feedback system to our thinking. If we change the way we think, we can take control over our emotions, or how we feel. Below highlights this scale by listing a range of emotions with the lighter better feeling emotions towards the top and the heavier more negative emotions towards the bottom.

1. Joy / Knowledge / Empowerment / Freedom / Love / Appreciation
2. Passion
3. Enthusiasm / Eagerness / Happiness
4. Positive Expectation / Belief
5. Optimism
6. Hopefulness
7. Contentment
8. Boredom
9. Pessimism
10. Frustration / Irritation / Impatience
11. Overwhelmed
12. Disappointment
13. Doubt
14. Worry

15. Blame

16. Discouragement

17. Anger

18. Revenge

19. Hatred / Rage

20. Jealousy

21. Insecurity / Guilt / Unworthiness

22. Fear / Grief / Depression / Despair / Powerlessness

Utilising the emotional guidance scale, at one end lies guilt and at the other end of the scale lays joy - two very different feeling emotions. If we start to move up the scale, anger would sit above guilt, not that we would want to stay there but it feels better to be angry about something than store guilt. Moving up again, frustration feels better than anger, as we start to move even further up we arrive at relief and then hope, each time feeling a little better. Let's use this emotional scale with examples of how we may respond to a particular golf shot. For this example we will use two very different feeling responses - **anger v curiosity.** For a moment, imagine the very first time you attempt something new. Perhaps it is studying a new subject, learning a new sport or starting a new job. You approach it with a degree of **curiosity, interest and an openness to learn**. You do not carry any negative patterns of thought or expectations from the past or hold fears of the end result but focus fully on embracing and learning in the moment as a newcomer. If you apply this to responding to a shot on the golf course or practice area, responding to a shot that may not have gone to plan with curiosity, it brings a solution oriented approach, a degree of optimism and in turn, a tension-free state. This tension free-state then provides an increased opportunity of a more successful platform and outcome on the following shot.

If we compare this to responding to a shot in **anger**, things may look and feel very different. There is a good chance it would be accompanied with a degree of tension, negative self talk and most importantly, is very likely to play itself out on the next shot or hole. How we respond to a triple bogey on a previous hole, how we feel about it and more importantly continue to feel about it will determine the success of what follows.

Of course, everyone is human and at times will respond to a shot in frustration/anger, the important factor is how long we hold on to that emotion. Ideally we have pre paved our emotional state prior to the shot and also as a result produced a greater chance of the shot more closely matching what we were after, however if a desired outcome is not attained, experiment with altering the emotional response and in this case, don't get mad, get curious! It is the change along the emotional scale these two states bring that makes the difference. In this instance, curiosity does exactly this in reference to moving up the emotional scale. It moves us from that fairly negative state of anger to a more neutral and positive feeling emotion which then automatically reduces physical tension. Any time physical tension is reduced on the golf course, the potential for a more technically proficient motion and improved result is increased. It also opens us up into a more positive, optimistic, forward thinking and solution-orientated response.

This example is not to be mistaken for analysing each and every shot, but simply assuming an air of curiosity, which in turn momentarily creates a better emotional state for the next shot and generates an opportunity for progression. Of course, you do not have to satisfy this curiosity alone and professional advice will help the process of gaining an understanding as to why the ball behaves as it does. However for the purposes of this chapter the key focus lies in the process of replacing anger with curiosity to alter your emotional state momentarily into a more positive and productive one. The temporary inquisitive state of questioning and intrigue creates a very different energy within you than if responding in anger. This then paves the way for a more relaxed and successful outcome, replacing what may have snowballed into a negative spiral of events. Momentum begins to move in a more positive direction. I do believe that once on the golf course, the aim is to get out there and simply play, not analyse things technically. However, if curiosity creates an avenue to release any emotional tension, along with an opportunity to move forward and further develop your game, it will certainly provide greater benefits than the tension filled response that accompanies anger. Curiosity is just one example of emotional responses, the key importance is to highlight how a subtle change in the emotional response, not the best thought or feeling imaginable, but a subtle shift which allows a change in how you feel both emotionally and physically.

Simply finding a thought that feels a little better and offers relief will set you on the right path. Ask the question, does this thought expand or contract me, do I feel lighter or heavier? Negative, fearful, tension based thoughts will tighten, contract and feel heavier. Thoughts moving in the direction of what we want, thoughts that support us will feel lighter and expand us. Technically a lighter and expanded physiology will be much more efficient than a contracted and restricted physiology and aside from the golf swing, it just feels better!!

> *'If it lights you, move in that direction. If it drains your life force, move away. Trust your internal GPS. Your body knows.' – Crystal Andrus*

Statements and corresponding feelings or emotions

In the figure below, on the left hand side is a repeated thought, statement or belief and on the right hand side is an example of a potential corresponding feeling or emotion that may accompany that thought, the exact descriptions of emotion may change according to the individual but the principle is based on the emotional guidance scale chart mentioned earlier in this chapter.

Statement/Belief	Potential Corresponding Emotion
I never putt well	⟹ Frustration, anger, despondency
I could putt well	⟹ Hopeful, optimistic, creative
I can putt well	⟹ Positive, optimistic, certainty
I am a good putter	⟹ Confident, relaxed state of belief and knowing
I am a great putter	⟹ Highly confident and a strong sense of knowing, belief

We need to create windows of opportunity that decrease the resistance and tension. Once we do so we are giving ourselves the best possible chance to create a positive outcome, or certainly a shot that is closer to what we were hoping for. Changing our language and thought process incrementally in a way which allows for an improved corresponding feeling, will begin to reduce any tension in the body and allow for an improvement in both our swing, shot and confidence. When we feel our way through the emotional scale, our inner guidance will always tell us when we slip off track; healthy thoughts feel good, detrimental thoughts feel bad, it is sometimes the simple things we end up ignoring!

Any time we create an improved emotional state, even if it is incrementally and provides some form of *relief*, we are moving closer to creating the shots we hope for and a more technically efficient golf swing; resistance and tension always hold them further away. The minute you think and feel your way into a state of relief you can almost physically feel a weight being lifted from your shoulders.

If there is a repetitive negative thought that often goes through your mind about your game whether it be putting, chipping, iron play or even your game as a whole, start to change your language and the words you use, feel the emotional changes along the way until eventually the more positive statement becomes the good feeling habitual thought pattern and belief. External circumstances and results will then begin to change.

Other ways of letting negative thoughts and feelings go

If you acknowledge a thought that doesn't serve you, you can experiment with simply letting it go and from there creating an opportunity of finding a better feeling replacement. Easier said than done I hear you say but with a little practice it will start to become a more natural process. Once you become aware and become the observer of the thought it creates the opportunity for detachment and a decision to release it. Within the field of Neuroscience becoming the observer of a thought is known as Metacognition. The frontal lobe is the seat of awareness within the brain, in the act of paying attention and becoming the observer of thought and who we are being it has the ability to act as a volume control. It can lower the volume of circuits linked to the old level of mind and fire new sequences, the brain then begins to seal circuits to the loudest thought. A substance called Neuro Growth Factor acts as a glue to seal the circuits, with only a certain amount to go around the strongest and loudest circuit steals the glue from neighbouring circuits eventually causing them to drift away. This enables the new pattern of thought to become more habitual.

A common theme throughout this chapter is that each time we make a positive emotional shift the chances of creating a technically more proficient golf swing and improved tactical decisions greatly improve. This is where in order to improve I believe it becomes almost impossible to separate the technical elements of a golfer from the power of their thoughts, emotions, and beliefs.

Another way of releasing a thought that doesn't serve us is to deliberately think about something completely different, something that holds no resistance and makes you feel good, it may have nothing to do with where you are on the golf course. Sometimes distraction is the path that offers the least resistance and will at the very least change your energy and release any built up tension. It may be a friend who always brings a smile to your face, the love of a family member or a loyal and loving pet. This doesn't mean losing concentration or focus on the golf course or during the shot itself. It simply provides the opportunity to create a positive internal energy shift and allow a more relaxed, better-feeling emotional state. If we keep focussing on the negative issue, the issue tends to grow. The more we ponder how badly things may be going, the worse we feel and the worse it seems to get. Spending time and energy on what is can only bring more of the same.

An inwardly relaxed and happy disposition will win hands down over four hours of anxious concentration. Even something as simple as an appreciation for being in the great outdoors, enjoying everything the golf course has to offer will create a different perspective and shift you into a better feeling emotional state.

> *'A leading difficulty with the average player is that they totally misunderstand what is meant by concentration. They may think they are concentrating hard when they are merely worrying'* – *Bobby Jones*

I remember well many years ago playing in an event, The Ladies British Amateur Championships, a main event on the Ladies amateur circuit. The front 9 was a torrid catastrophe of events, playing off a handicap of one at the time, I felt as though I had never picked up a golf club before, the centre of the clubface was not in the picture of things and I scrambled for dear life to get the ball in the hole in a respectable number. Things felt so awful that I literally wanted somebody to pick me up and take me away, anywhere, other than being on that golf course! I stood on the 10th tee (following another double bogey on the previous hole!) and quite literally in that moment chose to think and feel differently, I'd had enough. I didn't want to feel such tension and anxiety any longer, surely there had to be a better way! I chose to look around and take in my surroundings, a beautiful parkland course in central England, it was a lovely sunny day, blue skies and perfect summer temperatures. I was in good health and in that moment fully appreciated how lucky I was to be in that situation. From that point on I had made a crucial emotional shift, one that appeared not through trying or battling to find the most positive thought possible, but one that came simply through a conscious decision to change my perspective, appreciate where I was and the desire to feel better. I chose to look at the bigger picture and look at things in more general terms, gaining awareness and an appreciation for what *was* working. No more thoughts of lack, feeling inadequate to the task at hand or a panic that my golf swing needed fixing, but simply an appreciation of my surroundings and the opportunity that lay before me.

After absolutely no conscious technical swing changes on my part, the ball and the centre of the clubface were happily reunited and the back 9 flowed like a dream! Timing improved and everything felt effortless, I was actually enjoying myself! Unfortunately that back 9 was not enough to take any trophies home that week, but it did provide an extremely valuable lesson and learning curve and one that that has remained with me ever since!

Perspective can have a huge impact on performance and embracing a positive shift, whether it be inspired through a conscious decision for change or perhaps influenced through an experience or an event, can make all the difference. I have witnessed several times where students have had an experience that changed their perspective both in a generic sense and specifically around their game. Sometimes it can feel like we get caught in a loop of frustration and subsequently tension with regards to our game if things aren't going as we hoped. Once momentum builds in this state it can feel a tough one to pull out of. This is where perspective can make a significant impact and relatively instantaneously. I was working with a gentleman who had reached a good level of golf and attained a very solid 5 handicap. Under his own admittance over the years he had become overly analytical from a technical point of view and had reached a point where he was losing his love of the game. As a sports coach himself he had a natural instinct to deconstruct and analyse things technically, on the plus side very receptive to change, the downside being it can become a case of information overload where there is a constant breakdown of the golf swing. Unfortunately an accident at home caused a serious back injury causing 2 months of very limited movement and a year of not being able to hit a golf shot. The very first shot struck since the accident was during our coaching session together, unsure of how things would feel and if it was even going to be possible to continue to play golf again. Even though it was a very steady start it was very positive and things looked bright with regards to playing in the future. Aside from ensuring the pattern of movement within his swing wasn't putting undue stress on his body and the affected area within his back, a key element from the session became the understanding of how the overly analytical and at times self critical approach had created a stumbling block not only from an enjoyment point of view but also with regards to the consistency of his game. Reflecting back to a time where he was lying on his back after the accident simply hoping that one day he would be able to play golf again created a complete shift in perspective. This was an opportunity for a clean slate in his approach and thought process. The importance had now shifted from hitting the perfect shot to purely an appreciation of being able to hit a golf shot again, pain free and the opportunity to simply enjoy the game. This reflection could allow him to re-calibrate back to that moment in a positive sense and bring the focus back to an appreciation of where he now was compared to where he had been, this alone would make the process of the game far more enjoyable and hands down beat the analytical and critical approach which had taken him to the point of wanting to give up. The shift from critical analysis to appreciation created a big emotional shift, reducing tension and creating an opportunity for a more efficient golf swing, greater consistency and most importantly a more enjoyable experience in the process.

Another example comes from a student who also had an experience that led to a shift in perspective and one that dramatically changed his performance on the golf course. His wife had been particularly poorly and at one point the prognosis was fairly bleak. Thankfully over a period of time things improved and she was given a clean bill of health which was fantastic news. During his wife's illness he hadn't understandably played much golf, however once he returned, his first 3 rounds of golf were the best he had ever played and scored since he first took up the game and the upward spiral of this success continued. His perspective and focus had shifted, there was an overriding sense of the things he was thankful for, focus and pressure on the outcome or results within his game had shifted and in turn he felt happier and more relaxed on the golf course. From here he was playing his golf from a very different emotional set point and state of mind to how things had been previously which was then reflected in his performance.

Scientifically, the emotions of gratitude and appreciation have been proven to reduce the release of cortisol and stress hormones in the body. As cortisol levels go up a chemical called igA (immunoglobulin A) goes down. IgA is a protein and one of the strongest building blocks of life responsible for our internal defense system, our immune system. Reducing cortisol and in turn increasing igA brings health giving benefits. So not only is a shift in perspective (which subsequently creates an emotional shift) good for our game, it's also good for our health. A shift in perspective for the better can change everything, our enjoyment, our biology and ultimately our success on the golf course!

In relation to creating an emotional shift no matter how negative things may feel, relief can be one of the more easily accessible, positive and beneficial emotions available to anyone and one that provides a great stepping stone to improvement. Each of us has the potential to find a thought that offers a little relief. However we choose to do this, whether it be through becoming aware of and incrementally changing our language and thought process, releasing thought completely, or simply finding a more general, better-feeling focus, (general being *anything* that makes you feel better) improvements will always follow. In finding an improved feeling or emotion, momentum will begin to shift into a more positive direction; things then have to change. Greater results will show themselves through ease and enjoyment of the process; golf is supposed to be fun!! This is not to say that attaining our desires is void of dedication, focus or action, it simply means there is no need for it to feel like toil, effort or hardship.

> *'If you want to change the fruit, you have to change the roots. If you want to change the visible, you have to change the invisible first'.* – *T. Harv*

Logic versus emotions

Science also backs up the notion of the importance of emotion versus pure logic or thought void of emotion. The Institute of Heartmath have for the last 30 years studied the importance of the heart-brain connection and have measured the impact and role the heart and emotions play in what we think and experience. Their studies have shown that the heart is an electrical organ and produces an electro-magnetic field which measures up to 60 times greater in amplitude than the brain waves measured in an EEG. The magnetic component of the hearts field is 5,000 times stronger than the brain. The heart sends electrical signals to the brain and the body and produces an electrical and magnetic energy that can in fact be measured as a field surrounding the body up to 5-8ft. 2003 Dr Rollin McCraty Ph.D.

Research has shown that the natural beat to beat fluctuations in heart rhythm known as HRV - Heart Rate Variability, when measured, have been directly linked to distinct emotions. Regular sine wave patterns known as heart coherence are associated with positive emotions such as care, compassion, love and appreciation. Irregular and erratic heart rhythm patterns are linked to negative emotions such as frustration and anxiety. This electrical coherent or incoherent pattern sends a signal to the brain. The brain then responds by releasing corresponding chemicals into the body. An Incoherent signal from the heart causes the brain to release stress related chemicals into the body, a coherent signal sent to the brain releases life affirming chemicals, supporting the immune system and promoting healing. Optimal coherence is measured at 0.10 hertz and is seen to enhance benefits not only physiologically but also psychologically. The Institute of Heartmath states that heart coherence created through positive emotions, promotes a calm, emotionally balanced, yet alert and responsive state that is conducive to problem-solving, decision-making, and activities requiring perceptual acuity, attentional focus, and coordination. This would certainly provide a beneficial platform for a golfer to optimise their performance.

So, how do we attain this state of coherence, how can we create an optimal signal from the heart to the brain? As mentioned previously, four key emotions have been linked to this optimal coherent signal: Love, compassion, gratitude and appreciation. The Institute of Heartmath highlight that these states may be tapped into at any time through a simple, quick and effective technique known as The Quick Coherence Technique. It is a simple 1 minute technique that can be done anytime, anywhere.

Step 1: Focus your attention in the area of the heart. Imagine your breath is flowing in and out of your heart or chest area, breathing a little slower and deeper than usual.

Step 2: Make a sincere attempt to experience a regenerative feeling such as appreciation, love or care for someone or something in your life.

The hearts electro-magnetic field can not only impact our own internal state and chemistry but it can also radiate beyond our physical bodies, influencing both the electro-magnetic field and energy within the world around us and also other peoples electro-magnetic field. This suggests that the quality of our emotions and what we feel can greatly impact not only our performance on the golf course and general wellbeing but also our connection with others and the world around us.

Dr Joe Dispenza in his book, 'Breaking the habit of being yourself' also brings to light an experiment conducted by cellular biologist Glen Rein, Ph.D. where research highlights the importance of our feelings and emotions when held in conjunction with an intention or thought rather than simply thinking a thought separate of emotion.

In Dr Rein's experiment, he first studied a group of 10 individuals who were well practiced in using techniques that Heart-Math teaches to build heart-focussed coherence. They applied the techniques to produce strong elevated feelings such as love and appreciation, then for 2 minutes, they held vials containing DNA samples suspended in deionised water. When those samples were analyzed, no statistically significant changes had occurred.

A second group of trained participants did the same thing, but instead of just creating positive emotions (a feeling) of love and appreciation, they simultaneously held an intention (a thought) to either wind or unwind the strands of DNA. This group produced statistically significant changes in the conformation (shape) of the DNA samples. In some cases the DNA was wound or unwound as much as 25 percent.

A third group of trained subjects held a clear intent to change the DNA, but they were instructed not to enter into a positive emotional state. In other words, they were only using thought (intention) to affect matter. The result? No changes to the DNA samples.

Dr Dispenza summarises that the positive emotional state that the first group entered did nothing by itself to the DNA. Another group's clearly held intentional thought, unaccompanied by emotion, also had no impact. Only when subjects held both heightened emotions and clear objectives in alignment were they able to produce the intended effect. An intentional thought needs an energizer, a catalyst – and that energy is an elevated emotion. Heart and mind working together. Feelings and thoughts unified into a state of being. If a state of being can wind and unwind strands of DNA in two minutes, what does this say about our ability to create reality? 'Breaking the habit of being yourself – Dr Joe Dispenza

Be guided by your inner emotional compass, it is always with you and always letting you know where you are placing your focus, whether you are moving upstream or downstream, towards or away from your desire, it's the best companion you will ever have, on and off the golf course!

BELIEVING IS SEEING

'To believe in the things you can see and touch is no belief at all; but to believe in the unseen is a triumph and a blessing' – Abraham Lincoln, 16th President of the United States.

The power of belief holds an undeniable impact on the results we achieve not only on the golf course but also in our everyday life. The previous chapters began to highlight underlying belief patterns that may override our good intentions when *trying* to 'think positively'. The best golf swing in the world cannot override, on a long term basis, the power of belief if that belief is limiting or negative in anyway. In the same way the power of a positive belief and self-belief can assist greatly in creating all the results you want.

Maybe you have caught yourself thinking or saying, 'I don't normally win anything', 'I'm not very good at ball sports', 'I will never get a single figure handicap', 'I always go out of bounds on this hole', 'I am a bad putter' and so the list continues. If the deep-seated belief is a negative one, the unconscious mind will often create some way of sabotaging the desired result to fulfil the underlying belief system. In fact what we observe around us is very often not reality but patterns based on old beliefs, thoughts and emotions.

You may then think, 'If things on the outside changed I would change what I think', 'I will believe it when I see it!', 'I will believe I am a good putter when I hole more putts', 'I will feel confident I am a good player when I see the evidence of good shots.' Of course there is no denying that hitting a good golf shot or putt will instil greater confidence in a golfer and yes, a relatively sound technique will allow this to happen more consistently. However, if we constantly rely on external events and results to dictate our belief system and what we feel on the inside, there is greater potential for it to become more of a roller coaster ride of events, some good days, some not so good. It becomes harder to create a change and create what we truly want. You may have tried to make technical changes to your swing and the results only last for a short period of time and then you begin to feel that your golf gradually starts to go a little downhill? There may of course be other factors involved and repetition of a new movement with regards to change is key, however a primary contributing factor to this may be that the internal belief system has remained the same therefore things will potentially return back to their default position. The original negative belief will take precedence.

Many of our efforts are used trying to control things externally – our score, the wind, playing partners for example. When we get the inside right the outside begins to fall more effortlessly into place. (Effortlessly – with less effort, not devoid of effort!)

> *'Our limits are not where we think they are, you are only constrained by what you think you can't do, it bears no resemblance to the reality of what you can do'* - World champion triathlete, Chrissie Wellington

Creating new beliefs

The good news is that in just the same way a negative thought, and in turn a belief, may be repeated, a new pattern of thought and more positive belief which aligns closer to the desired goal can be created. Thoughts carry momentum. What this means is that a thought will naturally increase in momentum, by becoming aware of a thought pattern it creates an opportunity to decide if it is one that will benefit you as it increases in its momentum. If it is, and is one that serves you, it will develop into a positive belief system. Imagine a car at the top of a very steep hill, and you are pushing it from behind. If you try to stop the car at the top of the hill just before it is about to roll, you are in a far better position than trying to stop the car at the bottom of the hill, once it has built up speed and momentum. This example serves to highlight the momentum of thought, catch things in the early more subtle stages and we have an opportunity to guide things in a way that will benefit and align us in the direction of what is wanted.

If the thought feels good, build on the momentum of that good feeling thought. This is where it can be so important on the golf course to release a negative thought if the previous shot has not turned out quite as you want it to. If negative momentum builds, tension increases and creates a snowball effect on subsequent shots. Think of thoughts as a magnet, which then attract like thoughts to them. Awareness to these thoughts and emotions can create the link to any form of change. It is also key to note the importance of not berating yourself for any negative thoughts or feelings you may have but to acknowledge them without judgement and create a space that simply enables a break in the cycle. When there is an awareness of any thought patterns and beliefs that don't serve you, and you will know as they simply won't feel good as you think them, positive shifts can begin. A negative thought doesn't want to be seen as the big bad ogre but instead something that can be used positively as a bouncing off place. It is simply creating contrast between the wanted and unwanted; the choice then becomes to place greater focus on the wanted.

'Make a decision with such firm intention that the amplitude of that decision carries a level of energy that's greater than the hard wired programmes in your brain and the emotional conditioning in your body and your body has to respond to a new mind' – Dr Joe Dispenza.

The power of belief – The Placebo effect

One of the best examples of the power of belief is in the placebo effect. Scientific research provides evidence of the power of belief. For example, in medicine, when given a simple sugar pill to cure a medical condition, a patient has gone on to regain full health based on the *belief* that it was a medically prescribed drug.

A Baylor School of Medicine study, published in 2002, evaluated surgery for patients with severe debilitating knee pain. The lead author of the study, Dr. Bruce Moseley, 'knew' that knee surgery helped his patients: 'All good surgeons know there is no placebo effect in surgery.' But Moseley was trying to figure out which part of the surgery was giving his patients relief. The patients in the study were divided into three groups. Moseley shaved the damaged cartilage in the knee of one group. For another group, he flushed out the knee joint, removing material which was considered to be causing the inflammatory effect. Both of these constitute standard treatment for arthritic knees. The third group got 'fake' surgery. The patient was sedated, Moseley made three standard incisions and then talked and acted just as he would have during a real surgery – he even splashed salt water to simulate the sound of the knee-washing procedure. After 40 minutes, Moseley sewed up the incisions as if he had done the surgery. All three groups were prescribed the same postoperative care. The results were surprising. The groups who received surgery, as expected, improved. But the placebo group improved just as much as the other two groups! Moseley stated, 'My skill as a surgeon had no benefit on these patients. The entire benefit of surgery for osteoarthritis of the knee was the placebo effect'. Television news programs graphically illustrated the stunning results. Footage showed members of the placebo group walking and playing basketball, in short, doing things they reported they couldn't do before their 'surgery'. The placebo patients didn't find out until two years later that they had received fake surgery. – 'The Biology of Belief, Dr Bruce Lipton'

British hypnotist, illusionist and mentalist, Derren Brown conducted an experiment on the concept of the effects of placebo. He selected a handful of participants to take part, all of which had some form of fear or phobia they wished to get rid of. The experiment was based around a new 'fake' pharmaceutical drug that could help reduce fear within its recipients. Two of the participants included a gentleman who had a fear of heights and one who had issues with confrontation and self esteem. Everything around the event had been staged, the name of the drug, the professor issuing it and so forth. Following weeks of taking the drug, two scenarios were rigged to test the outcome of consuming what was purely a sugar pill. The gentleman who had a fear of heights was strapped securely to the outside of a very high bridge and gradually lowered over the edge. He proceeded to remain very calm, taking in his surroundings and even began to enjoy and admire the view! The gentleman, who had been fearful of confrontation, was placed in a situation, again completely staged unbeknown to him. A fight broke out in a pub just a few feet away from where he was enjoying a quiet drink. He promptly and calmly intervened to settle the situation down, showing no real signs of distress or anxiety. Both incidents were filmed and caught on camera to reveal the fascinating results. In both instances the participants had simply trusted the drug and as Derren states 'They had given themselves permission to act as if their problems didn't exist anymore'

This isn't to say we need to stand on a high bridge or intervene in a violent situation to prove the depths of our capabilities, it simply highlights the fact that everything comes from within us. Once the participants of the experiment had flicked the switch inside them and gave themselves the permission, releasing the old negative programmes they had developed, anything was possible. Nothing externally had changed, it had all happened internally through a change of thought, perception and belief.

> *'95% of the beliefs we have stored in our mind are nothing but lies, and we suffer because we believe all these lies' – Don Miguel Ruiz*

The power of belief within sport

The 4 minute mile was another classic example of the power of belief. It was universally believed that the mile could never be run in under 4 minutes until an athlete named Roger Bannister broke the barrier and ran under 4 minutes. Once that breakthrough was made more than 70 people broke the 4 minute barrier in the following 2 years. The belief was formed that it was possible, they now believed they could achieve it and they did.

In golf we can look at a similar instance in the rise of the young Korean golfer Se Ri Pak, who at the age of 20 in 1998 was the first Korean female to win a major tournament on the LPGA, winning the Ladies US Open. Since 1998 a Korean player has been named Rookie of the Year twelve times on the US Women's Tour having never won it a single year previous in the history of the Women's Tour. Today Asia's domination of the Women's Professional Tour continues to strengthen. Se Ri Pak initiated a new belief, the belief that it was possible for not only a Korean woman to succeed on the LPGA Tour but Asia as a continent could contend with the world's best female golfers.

Once there is the belief that it can be achieved, anything is possible, in the same respect that a limiting belief can also hold things away from you or certainly cause a delay. I had been working with a young player on the Ladies' European Tour who had been enjoying her second full season on the Professional circuit. She had a great result at the qualifying school where she gained her tour card, however success had been a little sporadic and halfway through her second season she felt she really wasn't fulfilling her potential and felt she kept tripping herself up when it really mattered. We talked things through and it came to the surface that she held an underlying belief that to win a tournament you needed to have had a successful season or at least played well from the outset. Her previous season hadn't quite been the fruitful one she was hoping for in reference to making cuts and overall performance and she had believed that you had to have had a good year to expect to be able to win an event. This was not a proven fact, simply, yet powerfully, a belief and perceived reality held in her mind and thought process. After our discussions, she had realised that this had been an underlying belief and one that was not a reality, but simply a reality that had been formed in her own mind which did not serve her. With the realisation of this limiting belief and the opportunity to release and replace it with a more empowering belief, it was almost as though a doorway opened. She gave herself the permission and opportunity to put herself in a winning position, no longer getting in her own way or taking the past out with her on the golf course.

A great example lies in the winner of the 2014 Ladies British Open, an American player named Mo Martin. Mo had started relatively late in the professional ranks and at the time of winning, was lying 99th in the order of merit with no previous record of winning an event on the LPGA Tour. On the final hole of the British Open Mo launched a 3 wood into the 18th green of a tough par 5 and promptly sank the putt for a tournament winning eagle. If Mo had any underlying belief patterns that suggested you needed successful wins or seasons before you could win a major event, there is an extremely high probability that the 3 wood or final putt wouldn't have turned out in the fantastic way that it did, the belief would have potentially sabotaged the outcome in some shape or form.

> *'There are no limiting beliefs, only plateaus – and we must not stay there, we must go beyond them'* –
> Bruce Lee

Think for a moment about what limiting beliefs you may hold about yourself both on and off the golf course. This is the negative internal dialogue that we convince ourselves is reality. We do so sometimes consciously, but very often unconsciously, so much so that it becomes a habitual habit. Limiting beliefs aren't always glaringly obvious, as they may have been habitually programmed in for many years. They are so automatic that we think it is reality of how things are. Even society places certain belief systems that condition us to think and believe in certain ways. If we open ourselves up to the possibilities and give ourselves the permission to contemplate the vision of our goals and dreams, anything is possible.

From the inside out

> *'Man is not limited by his environment, he creates his environments by his beliefs and feelings. To suppose otherwise is like thinking that the tail can wag the dog' – Emmet Fox*

Whether it is on the golf course or any other situation in life, we always have the opportunity to make a decision about our internal world, regardless of what is going on around us. If we allow our environment to determine how we feel, we are always at the effect side of life. In choosing to become at cause for how we feel internally and for choosing our emotions, beliefs and perceptions of a situation, regardless of what is happening externally, we not only have a much more enjoyable ride, but also begin to affect positively what is going on around us. If we can begin to develop the internal patterns of habits, beliefs, perceptions and feelings to match and ultimately create the outcome we desire, we begin to become the master of our performance, rather than the servant of our external world. The forthcoming chapters will explain and assist you in how to achieve this.

Embrace the opportunity of becoming the creator in your life experience. Don't wait for a good golf shot to determine how good you feel or a perceived poor shot to determine how frustrated or uncertain you feel. Only one thing determines how you feel, what you imagine, perceive and believe, and that's YOU!

THE GOLFING MIND – BREAKING THE PATTERN

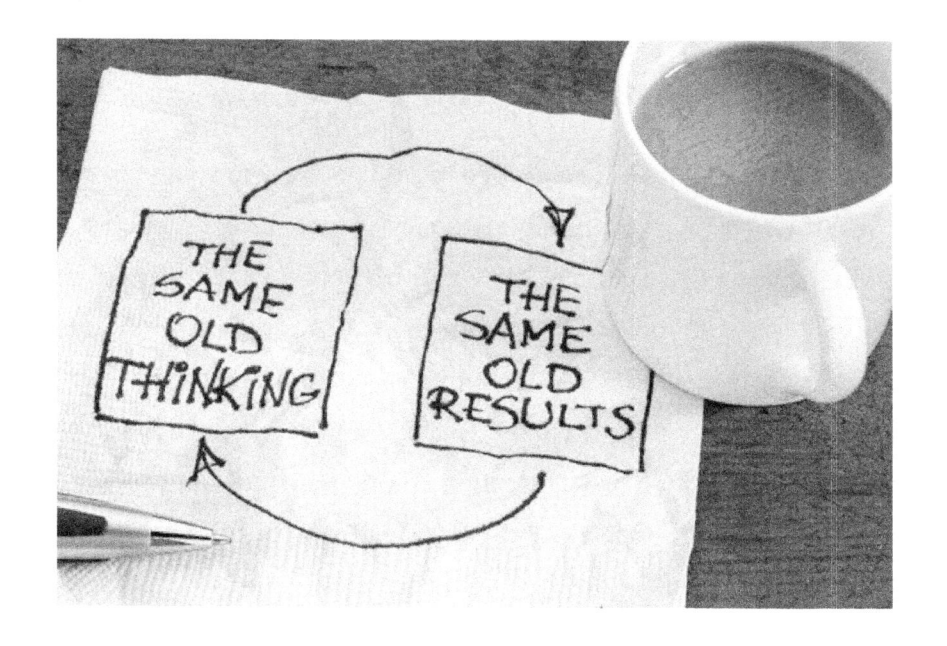

'If you're busy regretting the past, then a new future can't come in' – Marianne Williamson

The great news is that science now supports and has proven that the brain has the ability to create new neural pathways and change structurally through a change in thought patterns. The brain is a malleable organ, if we have a thought pattern that doesn't serve us, it can be changed.

'The brain holds a degree of neuroplasticity. 'Neuroplasticity is the ability to change the structure and functioning of the brain through experiences and the conscious use of directed thoughts' – Horizon Research Foundation.

So in fact the brain is not hardwired, we do not have to settle for 'that is just the way I am' or 'it's in my genes!' If we have a set belief or thought pattern that says 'I always perform poorly under pressure' or 'I always mess things up when someone watches me', or 'I'm not a natural sports person' whatever it may be, physiologically these neural pathways can be changed to a more positive and productive thought pattern. We have mentioned previously about changing beliefs and thought patterns but what really happens in the brain? There is now physiological proof that changes to the brain are being made.

The brain and neural pathways

Scientists now have evidence that you can create new neural pathways in the mind.

'Neurons and neural networks in the brain have the capacity to change their connections and behaviour in response to new information, sensory stimulation, development or damage'. – Centre for American progress.

The repetition of thought will imprint the information in your brain. With this in mind patterns of habit that don't serve us can be broken and replaced with more positive, beneficial and desire orientated thought patterns, creating new neural pathways and new outcomes.

> **'Neurons that fire together, wire together. To change the outer world, the inner world must change first. Break the unconscious habits to re wire the circuits of the brain' - Dr Joe Dispenza**

Imagine walking through a forest, it's a regular walk that you take on a daily basis. You follow the same set path, which over time through repetitive use has worn down into a defined pathway. At the end of the pathway is a pond which you see every day. It's not the prettiest of ponds, in fact, a bit grubby, but at least it feels safe on that route as you have been down it every day. One day you spot an opening that leads to a new route through the forest. There isn't much of a pathway, but you decide to follow it anyway. At the end of this new pathway lies a beautiful lake, crystal clear with stunning scenery you never even knew was there! You much prefer this lake and can't believe you put up with the old grubby one for so long! You make the decision that this will now become your new route and through daily repetition, it too eventually develops into a defined pathway in just the same way the old one did. Soon the old pathway becomes a distant memory, the grass grows over leaving little sign of where it once lay and you certainly don't miss that old murky pond! Think of the neural pathways in your brain as the pathway in the woods, the more you think a certain thought the more ingrained the neural pathway becomes, new ones can be developed and deepened, whilst old ones fade away.

To begin to break the old patterns of habit, we need to create new neural pathways and thought patterns. So often we operate on automatic pilot which allows any negative repetitions of thought to go unnoticed and we accept 'that is how I am'. Those negative thought patterns are generally old programmes from past experiences, if we are not consciously aware of them, we are simply allowing past experiences and thoughts to determine our present and future. Neuroscience supports the physiological change in the brain that happens during the process of changing old programmes once we become aware they are not serving us. **New thoughts, emotions and experiences will begin to make new neural pathways, neurocircuitry and the body's neurochemistry will begin to change.**

> *'The moment you change your perception is the moment you rewrite the chemistry in your body' –*
> *Dr Bruce Lipton*

Revisiting old thought patterns that no longer serve you mean that past experiences are tainting your present moment opportunities. If your brain is a record of the past and you don't have a vision of the future then you are living in the past and it difficult becomes difficult to create change and to arrive at the new future. This doesn't have to be the case. As Albert Einstein famously quotes,

'Insanity is doing the same thing over and over and expecting different results'.

Think of the old clothes that you keep in your wardrobe, some have been there for years without being worn. You either discard them to a charity etc or simply forget about them. They were useful at one stage in your life, maybe they were in fashion but you have now outgrown them. Imagine your old negative beliefs in the same light. You wouldn't dust off the old clothes every day, bring them out on display and show them off to people around you, yet this is what we sometimes do with our negative beliefs and stories about ourselves. The more we re-visit them on a daily basis, talk about them, share them with friends, the more we bring that story to life.

What old negative programmes have you been repeating that have consequently been holding you back on the golf course?

You may have found that you have been pleasantly surprised at how well you have played and enjoyed success on a new golf course, one which is less familiar than your regular club or course that you most often play on. This can very often be due to the fact that a new environment doesn't carry the old stories or patterns that we replay over in our mind of potential disaster scenarios on certain holes. It provides a clean slate and openness to possibilities each time we set up to the ball, there are fewer negative expectations which arise from simply bringing past experiences and patterns of thought into the present.

'By the time a person has reached the age of 35 they have memorised a set of behaviours, emotional reactions and thought patterns that have become 95% of their identity, the greatest habit we have to break is the repetition of the same routines carried out day after day. We begin to hardwire our brain into specific patterns that reflect our external world. To effect change we have to think beyond the environment and conditions in our life. If you allow the outer world to control how you think and feel, your external environment is patterning circuits in your brain to make you think 'equal to' your environment, which then creates more of the same.' Dr Joe Dispenza.

Research suggests that 5% of our waking state operates from the conscious mind and a staggering **95% operates from programmed old emotions in the body**. Each individual thinks approximately 60,000 – 70,000 thoughts per day, 90% of those are the same as the day before. Creating a clear intention of a new future or new outcome combined with a heightened positive emotion means the body and mind are now no longer living in the past or reacting to old unconscious programmes. The body doesn't know the difference between an emotion created by an actual experience or from one created by thought alone. Modern day science is now more than ever proving that change is always possible.

Why does change feel difficult?

Of course change can sometimes feel a little tricky. Thoughts and beliefs can sometimes feel difficult to break due to their previous repetition. There are times when a programmed habit is useful, i.e. when learning to drive a car or when a toddler learns to walk. Imagine having to relearn those things every day, fortunately after the initial learning stage the programme is set and it becomes an unconscious, repeatable habit. On the flip side, it is not so helpful when wanting to change a belief, habit or thought pattern that doesn't positively serve you.

Science also explains why physiologically, change can sometimes be difficult and highlights what is known as the **thinking and feeling loop** which conditions the body to repeat a certain thought. Each thought releases a chemical in the body, which produces a feeling. For example, happy, uplifting thoughts release chemicals, such as Serotonin and Dopamine, which produce corresponding feelings of joy and optimism, as examples. Thoughts of anger or fear release chemicals such as Cortisol, which produce corresponding feelings such as anxiety or frustration. The brain acknowledges the feeling and then creates similar thoughts to match the same feeling. This then produces more of the same chemicals and in turn feelings, creating a biochemical loop. At times the body can in fact become addicted to a certain chemical and feeling. It then becomes its default state and any other new feeling or thought trying to squeeze its way in can feel a difficult process. This helps to explain why it can at times feel easier to give up on change and slip back to the comfort zone and default position of the old programme, even if it is negative. So yes, change can feel uncomfortable at times. However, in just the same way we created the old programmes, science tells us that the brain and body will physiologically adapt, allowing any new thoughts to become a new automatic habit. Any unwanted negative thought programmes can be rewritten, rewired and re-programmed because the brain has the ability to change physiologically. What an empowering shift in perception and fantastic opportunity!

IMAGERY

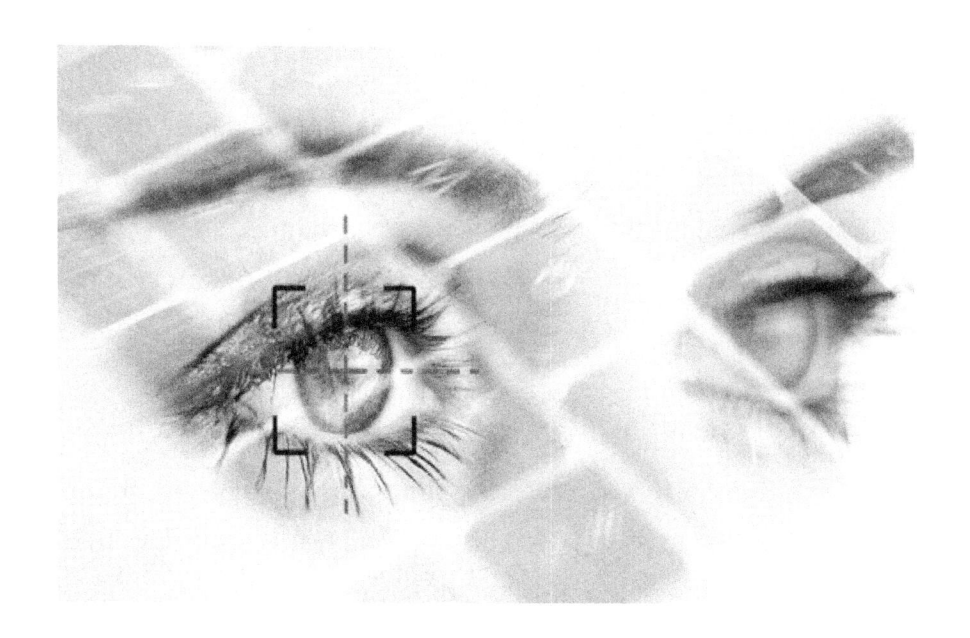

'Imagination is everything, It is the preview of life's coming attraction. Logic will get you from A to B, Imagination will get you everywhere!' – Albert Einstein

You will hear many of the great golfer's state how they will picture the flight of the ball and the shot they want to play in their mind; Jack Nicklaus described it in a way that he would never play a shot until he had seen the movie in his mind. The power of visualisation is undeniable. All the world's greatest inventors first had a picture of the end result in their mind before anything took its material form. The word 'imagery' is often used interchangeably with the word 'visualisation'. However visualisation suggests using only one of the senses (vision); imagery, on the other hand, relies on several senses including what you see, feel, and hear.

The subconscious mind is very receptive, and has no ability to reject a real or imagined event, it will simply accept it. If you create a picture in your mind and combine it with the corresponding emotions it will accept it as reality whether it is something wanted or unwanted, real or imagined.

The power of imagery

Imagine those worst case scenarios you may have pictured in your mind during a round of golf and think how many times you have lived up to those events as unwanted as they were. Maybe you pictured finishing the round off poorly, for example, or hitting it in the water on the final hole to shatter your chances of playing below your handicap? The flip side of this is that if these negative images have resulted in corresponding negative results, the exact opposite may be created by visualising and feeling the positive emotions of the results you DO want to achieve.

Think of the best shot you have played with a certain club. Perhaps it was a crisply struck 7 iron or maybe a perfect drive, long and straight down the middle. You can recall in your mind how the shot felt off the clubface. You can see the flight of the ball and you can recall all of the positive emotions that came with hitting the shot. You have it all stored there in your memory bank. We have access to recreating that state at any time and in doing so we have far greater chance of recapturing a similar outcome than if we imagine the worst case scenarios!

As a little exercise, close your eyes and imagine biting into a big juicy lemon. Really picture its colour, and imagine the sensations, making it as vivid as possible. In doing so I would take a guess that fairly immediately your salivary glands kicked into action and you created the same physiological response as if physically having the lemon right there with you. No lemon, just your imagination and a picture in your mind!

If you were to close your eyes and imagine being on holiday in your favourite idyllic place, the one place you hold extremely fond memories of, a place you truly love to be, again I would take a gamble that through these thoughts and images alone you could create all the positive emotions associated with the holiday as if you were there in person. Nothing externally has to change. If we flip this, negative situations can be remembered or imagined in exactly the same way. The point is that through imagination and imagery the emotional responses and corresponding physiological changes begin to occur whether the event is real or not. If our imagination begins to run away with us in a negative sense the same stress hormones are firing as if the event was really happening. Again potentially nothing externally has changed, only the vision inside your mind.

This is where on the golf course we have the choice and opportunity to either create positive visions for the present and future or replay disaster movies from the past (or imagined ones for the future!).

Consider this scenario: You have hit a tee shot which didn't go quite as you had hoped and you are now getting ready to take your approach shot. There is a large expanse of water between your ball and the green. Rather than berate yourself for the tee shot or worry about the water ahead, recall a great shot that you have played previously with the same club, what did it look like, how did it feel? Most importantly ensure there is a clearer visual of the intended shot and landing area rather than the shot you are drastically trying to avoid. Remember you have played many shots successfully in the past there is no reason why they cannot be recreated once again even if there is water to play over. **It's only your perception of the water that changes the situation.**

Imagery using all of our senses

So can the way we visualise have an impact on the results? The mind processes information through the five senses – Visual (seeing), auditory (hearing) Kinaesthetic (feeling), olfactory (smelling), and gustatory (tasting). These can translate into pictures, sounds, feelings, tastes and words (self talk). We can then break these down further into finer distinctions, which define the qualities of our internal representations; a few examples are as follows:

- **Visual: Making the image colour or black & white.**
- **Auditory: Making the sound loud or soft.**

A change in these finer forms of sensual awareness can create a very different feeling to a particular memory or thought about an event.

Think for a moment and picture your favourite film – eyes closed again! Now let's say you have pictured that film with colour, brightness and volume. It fills you with excitement, fun or whatever feelings the movie and your senses generate for you. Close your eyes once more. Now I want you to reverse what your senses translate. So from colour, change it to black and white. Make the picture dim and turn the volume right down. I'm sure your favourite movie now generates far less impact and creates very different feelings within you.

> *"I never hit a shot, not even in practice, without having a very sharp, in-focus picture of it in my head. It's like a colour movie. First I 'see' where I want it to finish, nice and white and sitting up high on the bright green grass. Then the scene quickly changes and I 'see' the ball going there: its path, trajectory, and shape, even its behaviour on landing. Then there is this sort of fadeout, and the next scene shows me making the kind of swing that will turn the previous images to reality." – Jack Nicklaus*

Associating with the image

Another process of imagery that can create a significant impact on your game is whether you are **associated** with the image or **disassociated**. If you are associated with the image, you are looking at the picture through your own eyes and experiencing the event using all of the senses, fully immersed. If you are disassociated it means you are looking at it from afar, there is a feeling of detachment. Imagine the difference between watching a television screen versus being inside the screen and in the programme itself! When you are disassociated you generally find it to be a slightly less intense experience.

Tiger Woods would admit to being able to use his creative mind and see shots all day long, it was only when he became more associated with the image and could also feel the shot was he then able to maximise on those creative shots.

From a personal point of view, I found this to make a huge impact on my game. I would often visualise the shot in hand, however I would do it from a disassociated and disconnected perspective, I wasn't fully engaged in the process, it was simply a procedure and process I felt that I 'should' be doing to improve my game. Due to not being fully immersed into the process there was still room for tension and negative thought patterns to creep in. It was only when I engaged other senses such as feel and sound, and fully immersed myself into the image – being fully present - did I begin to reap the rewards of visualisation and imagery.

Imagine visualising a simple trajectory line that you try to follow with your shot. You simply see the line. From a dissociated view point, it's purely a visual image. You are not immersed into the experience. Your brain will then go into overdrive, it will become cluttered in trying to find a way of matching that line, rather than utilising your own innate natural ability. If instead, you replace that with immersing yourself into the shot, being fully present, all of your senses are involved, yes you have a visual of the shot but now you can actually feel the process too. You are allowing your natural ability to create the shot. There is no clutter or mechanical thought process, simply a relaxed trust; it can be pleasantly surprising how much your body can respond instinctively if you allow it to.

You may recall a similar feeling whist setting up to a putt and certain times where you having a very clear uncluttered focus and visual of the putt and a knowing that you are going to hole it. The ball then willingly complies!

Experiment with imagery. Use as many senses as you wish. Intensify the experience and always make sure the intensified image is of the shot or scenario you want, not the disaster movie you are drastically trying to avoid. Take time to visualise the shot you wish to play. As part of your pre-shot routine stand behind the shot and create a positive focus of where you want the ball to go rather than the hazards you are trying to avoid. Really associate and immerse yourself into process of that positive image. Focussing on the part of the fairway you want to hit or the area of green you wish to land will produce a far greater chance of arriving there than focussing on the bunker you really don't want to land in or the trees on the left you are drastically trying to avoid! Commit to creating a positive focus of what you wish to achieve and you have a much greater chance to attaining it.

> *'Visualisation is the most powerful thing we have as golfers'* – *Nick Faldo*

Imagery and the pre-shot routine

> *'Golf is a lot like life, when you make a decision, stick with it'* – *'Byron Nelson'*

One thing you will notice when watching the players on the professional tour is that they will all have a routine that they carry out before every shot and each one will contain some form of imagery and visualisation process. The full routine and technique may differ but they will all commit to a pre-shot routine before every shot, even under the most pressurised of situations. To ensure consistency with all shots it helps to create a consistent pre-shot routine. Ideally the routine will remain exactly the same and take roughly the same amount of time before each shot. It is important to include the routine in **all types of golfing situations and scenarios** whether it is a friendly 9 holes or the final shot into the green during a tournament. This way it will become an automatic part of your game whether on the golf course or the practice area and will serve you well in any pressurised situations, replacing any urge to panic or rush the shot.

A good routine will ideally include the following steps:

1) **Confirmation** in your mind of the intended shot.

2) A **compelling image** of the intended shot, utilising all of the senses.

3) A practice swing **replicating the actual shot ahead**.

4) A **positive affirmation** of the shot - no last minute thoughts of the shot you want to avoid!

5) Stepping into the shot **fully committed**.

Imagery and a pre shot routine will reap its full rewards when undertaken with complete immersion and a commitment to the process. If accompanied with doubt or anxiety the potential for successful results greatly diminishes. When you are in complete harmony, physically, mentally and emotionally, the benefits of imagery become a reality and golf becomes a more enjoyable activity in the process.

> *'Be decisive. A wrong decision is generally less disastrous than indecision' – Bernard Langer*

THE FEAR FACTOR!

> *'Our eyes are not only viewers, they are also projectors, running a second story over the picture we see in front of us, fear is writing that script'* – *Jim Carey.*

How is it we can hit balls on the range with ease and success, yet we head on to the course and everything feels completely different, as if our arms are, at times, not connected to our body?! Or we strike the ball crisply out of the middle when out playing a relaxed 9 holes with friends or when we head out to play a few holes on our own. Yet we enter the monthly medal or an important tournament, and the centre of the club face seems to have packed its bag, left the building and vanished completely?! The culprit is often based around fear - in particular, the **fear of a perceived negative consequence**.

Whenever golf is played from a position of fear it creates a barrier to maximising potential. Of course, one person's perception of a fearful situation may be very different from another. A tournament scenario may spell fear for one golfer but fill another with excitement and anticipation - the same reality, but a very different internal representation and perception of the event, in turn, producing a different emotional state and behaviour.

Fear on the golf course

Fear will potentially arise on the golf course whenever there is some form of perceived negative consequence involved. There can be several perceived reasons to be fearful, however as a whole, they will often, in varying degrees, stem from some form of fear of failure. Each individuals experience may be different, however in general, underlying reasons are often rooted in:

- **The fear of being judged**
- **The fear of falling short of expectations – both of self and others**

The fear of failure

Very often the fear of failure can be at the heart of what prevents us from pursuing our goals or allowing our true potential to shine through and can at times create a roadblock to success. Fear of failure simply means greater energy and focus is being placed on the exact outcome we are desperately trying to avoid. Focus is either ahead in time and on the future, or in the past, playing back a previous unwanted event, hoping not to repeat the same outcome. It is not, as it ideally wants to be, involved with the present moment. It is important to remind ourselves that there is in fact no failure, only feedback. If our mind spirals into any imagined circumstances of failure (and often they are all imagined as they haven't happened yet) the key lies in bringing our awareness back to the present moment, becoming aware of how we are feeling in that moment in time and where we are placing our focus.

The fear of being judged

Holding a perception of being judged very often brings with it a degree of resistance and tension, playing from here can only create blocks between you and what you know you are capable of. Think of those times where you have gone out for a relaxed 9 holes with a good friend who you regularly play with and feel comfortable with, knowing that they hold no judgements over you whatsoever. It feels as if everything just flows, it feels easy. You are free from any tension, there lies no fear in any consequence or fear of being judged, there are no external pressures.

Sometimes it becomes human nature to begin to assume, predict or mind read what other people may be thinking. We may assume that others are judging us in a negative light, when many times the assumption is, in fact, way off the mark. Most often, people are focussed with their own games and performance, they know only too well that this great game can at times be a little unpredictable and there leaves little time or space for judgement on others! If it is any consolation, it can often be the case that if people are judging others, beneath the surface they are potentially holding themselves in judgement in equal or greater proportions!

Your enjoyment of the game is the top priority and caring about the way you feel holds far more importance above anything externally. Eliminating your fear of being judged creates a platform to play golf with freedom, allowing your natural ability to shine through. You cannot control what others think or feel. The greater priority you place on other people's thoughts and judgments, the more it is diverting you away from utilising your own natural ability and enjoyment of the game. We cannot control the thoughts or actions of people around us. One thing we do have complete control of, is our own internal experience. Nobody can disrupt that, unless of course, we give them permission to do so.

> *'There are more scary things inside than outside' –*
> *Toni Morrison*

The fear of falling short of expectations

Berating yourself for falling short of any expectations you have placed on yourself or expectations you feel are placed on you from others can once again create a block to allowing that free flowing, effortless golf that you know is in there and have felt many times in the past. Imagine a young child learning to play golf, or aspiring one day to join the ranks of their favourite golfing heroes. Imagine what you would say to them were they to make a mistake, should they three putt the third green, catch the water on the right, or have, what they feel is a poor 9 holes. My guess is you would encourage and nurture them in a way that they would want them to dust themselves off and get back to the job at hand. You wouldn't berate them or hurl a barrage of name calling at them, which is unfortunately the approach as adults we sometimes take on ourselves. You must encourage yourself in exactly the same way you would a young child, and in doing so produce an outcome far more aligned to your goals and desires than a barrage of abuse and negative self talk ever would.

You really do need to be your own best friend out on the golf course. You are only ever doing the very best you can in any given moment and it is important to remind yourself of this often. Words of support and encouragement such as 'I am doing the very best I can at this moment', or 'I played that hole well under the circumstances, I made a really good decision with that final approach shot' will not only create a very different and more relaxed physiology, but most importantly a far more enjoyable experience. Berating yourself for feeling that you have fallen short of the mark either by yours or somebody else's standards only holds you further away from truly fulfilling your potential.

Fight or Flight

Let's look at the 'fight or flight' response and its role when dealing with fear. Imagine a gazelle merrily grazing in its natural habitat in the wild. Within minutes of happily grazing, a predator is launching its attack. The gazelle makes a mad dash, escapes with its life and within a few minutes of the terrorising attack goes back to merrily munching its lunch, having notched up a bit of an appetite whilst running frantically for its life! Its fight or flight response has automatically kicked in to save itself from a life or death situation. As humans, we also have this in built fight or flight mechanism. Unlike animals, human beings' fight or flight response kicks into action not only in life and death situations but also in how we deal with everyday stresses and fears both on and off the golf course.

The "fight or flight response" is the body's primitive, automatic, response which prepares the body to fight or flee from a perceived attack, harm or threat to survival. In the case of the gazelle, its fight or flight system kicked in to save its life and the gazelle then went back into its normal state, happily grazing away. Any onlooker would have never known that 20 minutes earlier it was darting for its life. This is where humans begin to differ. As humans, the fight or flight system releases stress hormones and chemicals into the body, such as cortisol and adrenaline, which create a response in the body to prepare itself for the perceived threat. Physiological changes that occur, amongst other symptoms, include increased heart rate, dilating pupils and blood flow being directed to the skeletal muscles. The key here is that as humans we generally (and thankfully) don't have to run from a sabre tooth tiger or predator from the wild too often, that is, from life and death situations. However, we perceive certain situations that can still trigger the exact same chemical reaction. The hypothalamus and amygdala (the primal regions of the brain, associated with fear and emotion) do not know the difference between a bounced cheque, teeing up on the 18th to win the club championship or running from that sabre tooth tiger!

In addition, unlike the gazelle we may be affected by the fight or flight mechanism well after the event has happened, in the form of continued anxiety and stress. This then places the body constantly in a mode of defence as it is always on the lookout for that perceived threat. When the body is in defence mode there leaves no room for growth. After a period of time the body can then begin to show signs through physical symptoms or illness in various ways. This in turn means that being in a constant state of anxiety and fear, if left unchecked, can not only inhibit improvements and enjoyment within our golf but also impact our overall wellbeing.

Unfortunately, often a great a deal of time can be spent anxiously fearing the very things we are trying to avoid on the golf course! We fear the trees on the left or the water on the right, going in the bunker or finishing in last spot in an event, maybe even blowing up on the last hole in view of everyone watching from the clubhouse!

Scientific research demonstrates the benefits of adopting a more positive-oriented thought process and show that positive, expansive emotions such as optimism and excitement, release different chemicals, such as oxytocin and serotonin, which naturally shuts off receptors in the amygdala and in turn, the body's stress response. If we consider that the stress response affects not only our physiology but also our decision making process on the golf course this would be a very beneficial component to our performance.

> *'Of all the hazards, fear is the worst'* – *Sam Snead,*
> *7 time major championship winner.*

Why an earth did I do that?!

Have you ever questioned those moments where, when anxious and under pressure, you perhaps haven't made the wisest of decisions? Those times where maybe you knew deep down on that 3rd attempt, you really should have taken an iron off the tee and not fired another driver out of bounds!

If so, this may help make things become a little clearer! Let's delve a little deeper into what happens during those moments when under stress, and the fight or flight response kicks in.

The stress response releases the fight or flight adrenal hormones into the bloodstream. This constricts the blood vessels of the digestive tract and redistributes the blood and energy to the limbs, allowing us to flee or fight. The immune system also shuts down to conserve energy reserves. Fighting off a stomach bug takes secondary place when faced with escaping from that sabre tooth tiger! (This also why we can get colds etc when we are run down or stressed)

The processing of information in the forebrain (conscious mind), which is the centre of reasoning and logic, is significantly slower than the reflex activity controlled by the hindbrain (subconscious mind). Think how quickly you react when you step back on to the curb if a lorry is hurtling down the road. This is the quick reacting and instinctive hind brain in action. A logical, deliberate decision-making process would not be ideal under those circumstances. In an emergency, the faster the processing of information, the more likely of survival. Blood flow to the forebrain is redirected to the hindbrain, which is the quicker processing system. While good for survival, it also diminishes conscious awareness and reduces intelligence. This is why in perceived fearful situations, and when under stress, we don't always make the wisest of decisions and logic seems to go out of the window! That tiny gap through the trees seems to have your name written all over it, playing out safely sideways does not get a look in! When under stress our focus narrows as we single out and prioritise the one thing needed to survive, we are less able to access our higher reasoning or consider any alternative, more suitable options. So fearless golf is not only good for your performance and results but is also key in decision-making processes.

How can fear show itself on the golf course from a technical perspective?

Aside from the impact of excessive tension as detailed in previous chapters, let's take the following example of a scenario on the golf course. You are standing on the 17th hole of an important tournament with a good scorecard in your hand. It is a par 4 with water running along the right hand side of the fairway. You decide to pull the driver out of the bag; standing on the tee all you can think about it is avoiding the water on the right hand side. You know in your mind you have been playing well, unfortunately you have now started to calculate what you need to score on the last few holes to play under your handicap or of potentially doing well in the event, subsequently you become fearful of going in the water and blowing your chances. There are a number of things that can happen to the golf swing technically whilst in this fear based scenario. Very often when we are fearful of something we tend to put a great deal of focus on trying to move away from it, unfortunately this still means we are putting a large proportion of energy into the very thing we are trying to avoid! In this situation with the main focus being the fear of the water, the first instinct is to aim the body well left of the hazard (based on a right handed golfer) This is not necessarily a bad thing however if overdone or done incorrectly problems can arise. Let's take an example where the shoulders are pointing dramatically left of the ideal target line, traditionally classed as being too open. The natural tendency can often be for the hands and arms to follow the line of the shoulders and pull across the ball through impact. If the hands follow the line of the arms and shoulders and release, the ball will generally go left. However if instinct kicks in and we try to prevent this from happening by not allowing the hands to release and we hold the clubface open (aiming right of target, or aiming right in relation to the swing path/direction the club is being swung) through impact, the right side of the course will potentially now come in to play. Combine this with the often subconscious tendency of trying to drastically turn the body away from the hazard during the downswing and it unfortunately encourages more of the shot we are trying to avoid. In turning the body through the shot excessively in an attempt to pull away from the hazard on the right, the hands and arms get left trailing behind. The club is then left generally trailing behind the body and the clubface potentially pointing to the right at impact (again based on a right handed golfer). A rather long winded explanation admittedly but in summary all coming from our instincts of trying to avoid what we fear! If we replace that with a positive focus on the target and where we want the ball to land rather than fear of where we are trying to avoid, we will generally produce a more relaxed and technically proficient golf swing and one more in line with our own natural ability. The hands, arms and body will swing positively towards the intended target. With improved timing (resulting from a less volatile thrust of the body away from the hazard during the downswing) the hands, arms and body will become more in sync. This will allow more pressure to be delivered on the ball and increase the potential for the direction of the club path and clubface to be more on line with the chosen target, ultimately increasing the chances of the ball landing where we **want** it to go and not where we are trying to avoid. There are of course variables to the above scenario however it is simply to highlight the importance of where we place our attention and the potential impact it can have on our swing from a technical perspective.

Why didn't I do that the first time?!

> *'Every time you are focussing on your fear it is moving you further away from your desire. Fear is resistance to a negative outcome, you don't want something to happen so you take control away from your natural ability. When your fear is stronger than your vision, you will try to control the outcome. In this situation your outcome will more closely resemble what you fear than what you want.' Dr Tim Kramer*

A provisional ball is our second bite of the cherry, if a shot goes into trouble and we think it may never be found again we reload with a second ball and attempt. Many golfers find their provisional ball goes exactly where they intended the first time around. The wise words above from Dr Tim Kramer help to explain why this can happen and those times where the provisional ball sails straight to the intended target, the exact replica of the shot that was desired initially! If we use the example of the previous paragraph with regards to fearing the out of bounds or trouble on the right, the vision and focus on the hazard will potentially be stronger than the vision of the desired shot. Consequently, there would be a greater temptation to control the outcome rather than trusting your natural ability. The second time around with a provisional shot, you would potentially be more relaxed and care free as the worst case scenario had already happened. The fearful images and internal chatter would fall away leaving a clear image of the desired outcome you first had in mind and hey presto, your natural instinct and ability came into play and the result appears!

Other similar scenarios may include tournament situations versus a relaxed 9 holes with friends, driving range practice versus playing on the course, or even when a fourball have waved you through and you feel the pressure of being watched. Anytime you're fearful focus and vision of the unwanted is greater than the desire, the chances of achieving your ideal outcome are greatly decreased. You will always know when you are steering more in the direction of what you fear. Your emotions and bodily sensations will tell you through various feelings of anxiety, negativity and tension. Fear is always accompanied by those stress-releasing chemicals in the body which create the uncomfortable feelings of anxiety and tension. The moment you heighten your awareness to this, you begin to allow an opportunity for change. Whenever you feel any form of tension in your body, it is a little nudge to let you know that you are potentially beginning to place greater focus on your fear. Staying in the present moment allows you to gain the awareness and shift your focus into a more positive direction. Awareness is the key! Helpful ways of achieving this will be discussed in the following chapter.

The following exercise can also assist is creating greater present moment awareness:

Imagine standing over each shot and simply being aware that all you need to do is get that ball from A to B every single time you play the shot. No drifting ahead, no fearing the outcome, no thoughts of calculating the end score and no fear of judgement from others.

Simply focus on the present moment each time you set up over the ball and getting it, shot by shot, from A to B. It may take a little time initially as the mind will want to wander but stick with it and you will begin to not only see improvements in your game but also the capacity to enjoy your round greatly increases.

To summarise, we know that fear, anxiety and stress do not serve our golf swing, our games as a whole, or in fact our wellbeing. The more we can place a greater emphasis towards what we want rather than avoiding what we fear on the golf course the greater the enjoyment and potential for improved performance. We have our own in built fight or flight mechanism designed to protect us in any, hopefully rare, moments of danger, with this in mind rest assured that nature has got it covered!

> *'Focus on where you want to go, not on what you fear'* – **Tony Robbins**

EAST MEETS WEST – BREATHING, PHYSIOLOGY & MR MIYAGI!

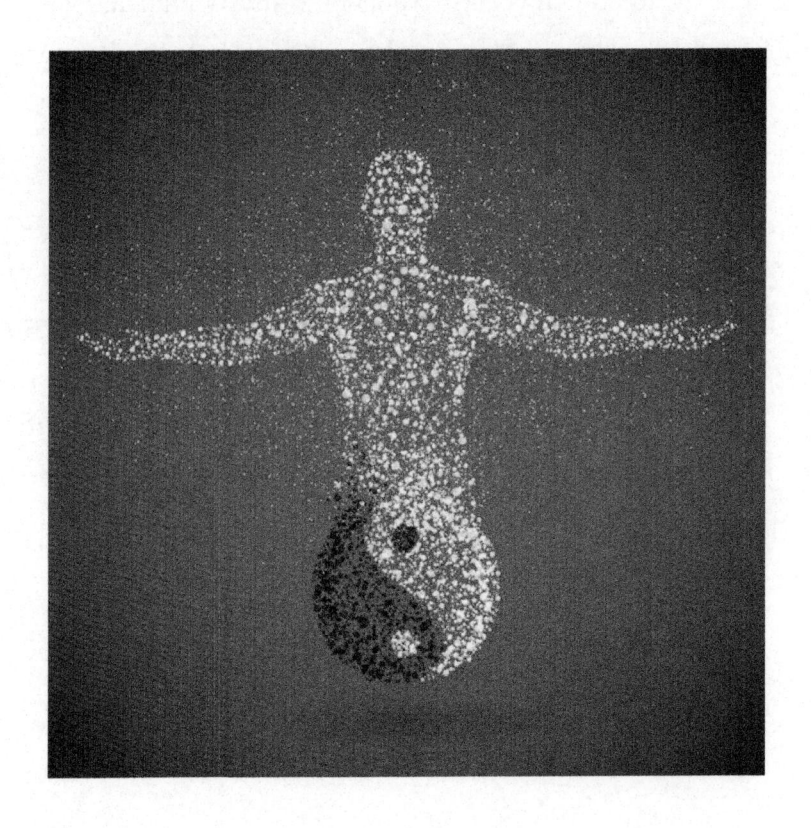

'If you know the art of breathing, you have the strength, wisdom and courage of 10 tigers' – **Chinese adage**

Following on from the example in the previous chapter we can look a little further into how negative thoughts or emotions can translate themselves into a shot soaring out of bounds on a certain hole! Speaking technically, the physical by-product of negative emotion manifests itself as tension in the golf swing. From a swing efficiency point of view this can be fairy destructive. We understand that tension in the grip generally works its way up through the arms, shoulders and upper body. This can greatly impact the body's ability to move and rotate efficiently and can have a tendency to force the club out of position (rather than allowing natural forces to assist in the process). It also reduces maximum club head speed potential.

Some of the Eastern philosophies and martial arts practices, I believe, offer great foundations to the golfer. In order to move efficiently and produce maximum power with minimal effort, martial arts practitioners would hold a centred and balanced posture, a stable lower half, whilst maintaining a relaxed upper body. They breathe from their lower abdomen or what they call the **Dan T'ien** (positioned just below the belly button) with deep diaphragmatic breaths. Power, speed and energy are released through the exhalation. They would never attempt to create speed or efficiency through tension or in fact holding their breath until the move is complete. These are some of the factors that allow highly experienced practitioners to take on feats that in logical terms would be impossible to complete successfully, whether that be breaking through planks of wood with their bare hand or taking on opponents twice their height, frame and strength. They are channelling their energy extremely efficiently. The basis of these principles would certainly assist the golfer. In martial arts, the angles within the posture and starting position are of course a little different, but the remaining principles would certainly create a good picture for the golfer looking to achieve successful results.

A popular film originating in the 1980's, Karate Kid, had a main character called Mr Miyagi. Mr Miyagi was an older small-framed gentleman who trained a young boy how to follow in the footsteps of a martial arts master. Mr Miyagi did not have youth, height or a power house of muscular strength yet his ability to produce effortless speed and power outshone opponents many years his junior. Instead he relied on a calm and centred focus, a stable posture and efficient breathing. This allowed him, combined with a repetitive discipline, to create all the strength, speed and power he needed to take on any opponent who so chose to stand in his path. Applying the principles of Mr Miyagi and the martial arts world of deep breathing and centeredness would certainly help the golfer in creating effortless power and the opportunity of producing a relaxed, yet efficient powerhouse.

Breathing

With regards to breathing, generally, the golfer when under pressure, will tend to create short, shallow breathes from the upper body and chest. This can unfortunately create added muscular tension in the upper body, a by-product of which can lead to a less efficient golf swing. The ability to create an efficient body rotation can be compromised.

Having an awareness of your breathing and any built-up tension is the first important factor. When you become aware of your breathing you are then able to create an alternate and more relaxed state. In golf, tension can often go unnoticed.

So can being aware of my breathing really help me hit more fairways?!

As mentioned previously there are several potential consequences resulting from excessive tension, however below offers another example highlighting how a negative thought process has the potential to affect physiology (muscular tension), which in turn affects the technical components of the golf swing and ultimately the ball flight.

If the upper body becomes tense, frequently linking in with shallower breathing patterns, it can often become dominant over the lower body, the lower body can then become less of a platform or base. A tense and more dominant upper body has greater potential to initiate the transition into the downswing, generally causing the path of the club to travel from out to in or left of the target (for a right handed golfer). This combined with tension in the grip makes it very difficult to produce a natural release of the clubhead through impact. Depending on what the hands do at impact and where the ball is struck on the clubface, either side of the golf course could come in to play in this scenario. Distance may also be affected and reduced.

The benefits of focussing on your breathing are twofold. Firstly, the relaxation of the muscles generated from correct breathing, (from the abdomen as mentioned above), creates an awareness and a contrast in how much tension over time has potentially accumulated in the body. Often we do not realise how much muscular tension we are holding on to until we release it with a few deep breaths. With that awareness in place and a more relaxed physiology there is a far greater opportunity of creating a more technically efficient movement in the golf swing. When the upper body is relaxed it has a greater opportunity to create an efficient rotary movement when supported by a relatively stable lower body, enabling the potential for increased club head speed with far less effort.

Breathing correctly also allows you to create greater present moment awareness, which allows you to focus purely on the shot in hand in a relaxed positive state, taking you away from perceived fearful thoughts and situations. Think of the times where maybe you have had a good scorecard going and you were having a really good round. You then started to get ahead of yourself and tried to finish the round off in your mind, thinking what scores you would need on the remaining holes to play below your handicap or finish with a really good score! In this scenario focus has been taken away from the present moment which means it becomes harder to give the current shot in hand your full focus. Tension creeps in, you get a little anxious, maybe you start to doubt your capabilities or don't believe you are good enough to achieve that end score you have your mind set on, you start to focus on the perceived fearful consequences. Whatever thought it maybe, it is clouding your ability to give your very best to that particular shot in hand. Being aware of and taking control of your breathing can bring you back into the present moment, enabling you to focus solely on the process of the current situation and shot in hand.

> *'Be aware of your breathing. Notice how this takes attention away from your thinking and creates space'* – Ekhart Tolle.

Tiger Woods maintains that in the moments on the golf course which are more intense, he is so encompassed in the here and now that he actually feels as if things are slowing down and he feels calmer. 'The last few holes seem to take forever!' He also describes the times where he doesn't hear noise or can remember what is going on around him, 'I become so enthralled in the moment.'

This may be a very different scenario from certain intense moments you may have found yourself in on the golf course where a thousand and one thoughts are racing through your mind, your grip pressure has doubled and your heart is beating ten to the dozen!

Studies have also shown the physiological benefits of deep breathing and how it affects the bodies stress response.

'Deep diaphragmatic breathes interrupt the 'fight or flight' stress response. It allows more oxygen into your lungs and blood stream, enabling your muscles to have more 'fuel'. It also causes the heart to beat more slowly and with less effort. The amazing and complex interplay between the brain and the various hormone-producing parts of the body will change when you practice deep breathing and smaller amounts of stress hormones will be released. The liver and kidneys will then be able to 'catch up' with all of the stress hormones in the blood stream and the fight or flight response decreases and ultimately stops' – CMHC UT Counselling and Mental Health Centre.

Ultimately an awareness of and incorporating healthy breathing patterns provides the added bonus of a more technically efficient, tension-free golf swing, combined with the opportunity for that present moment focus and clutter free mind.

> *'As we focus on the breath, we slow down the unwanted chatter inside the mind. We cannot, after all, tap into emotions of anxiety and calmness in the same moment in time. Then, as we slow down the chatter, we soften unwanted tension and resistance in the body. We gain immediate access to an infinite stream (flow) of energy – The Zone – of which no other state of peak performance compares.'* – Dr Tim Kramer

How to practice deep breathing

There are several resources and variations of breathing techniques available. Here is a simple deep breathing exercise.

Breathe in slowly and deeply through your nose. Let your stomach fill with air. If you were to place one hand on your chest and one hand on your stomach, the hand on your stomach should rise more than the hand on your chest. As you exhale feel your abdomen lower and push out as much air as you can while contracting your abdominal muscles. You will feel a sense of relaxation in the shoulders, chest and upper body. Repeat several times.

Once you are able to feel the difference between the short shallow upper body breaths and the deeper lower abdominal breaths you are then in the driving seat, that awareness alone can begin to make a big shift. You can take deep diaphragmatic breaths on the golf course in-between shots, during a pre shot routine, just prior to hitting a shot, or at any point where you feel a degree of tension or anxiety creeping in.

Mindfulness

> *'Active noticing and embracing of experience in the here and now.'*

Creating greater present moment awareness allows the opportunity to focus on each shot in the now, creating the space to start afresh every time you set up to the ball. Your last shot or round is simply a reflection of the emotions developed prior to that moment; present moment awareness of the breath and the now, allows you the opportunity to provide a new, more empowering emotional platform for what lies ahead.

Mindfulness is simply the **practice of paying attention** – paying attention to what is happening in the present moment with acceptance and without judgement. Being mindful is like practicing meditation while at the same time moving around and engaging in your daily activities. You do everything you would normally do, but you experience each activity fully, with all five senses. You tune in to what you're doing now, rather than focusing on what you did yesterday or what you'll be doing next. You pay attention to your thoughts and your feelings. Over time, mindfulness will enable you to place your attention where you want it to be and when you want it. It will become a helpful habit and definitely a useful habit to have on the golf course. Mindfulness training is fast becoming a valuable mental tool that athletes can use to help overcome any unwanted thoughts or feelings during a competition.

Even being mindful and having a physical awareness of where the clubhead is during the golf swing can bring benefits. Feeling the weight of the clubhead and utilising natural forces rather than the swing being carried out with such speed and tension there is little sensation or awareness of where the clubhead is at any point during the shot.

Research has been carried out into the effects of mindful meditation. MRI scans showed after an eight week course of mindfulness practice, the art of reflection and quietening the mind, the brains 'fight or flight' centre, appears to physically shrink. As the amygdala shrinks, the pre-frontal cortex of the brain, which is associated with higher order brain functions such as awareness, concentration and decision making, becomes thicker. These are certainly beneficial by-products and would be of great value to performance.

Meditation

There are many different ways to meditate whether it be focussing on your breathing, guided meditation or focussing on a mantra, as examples. The key essence of the practice is ultimately to quieten the mind, relax and release the stressors of the day or life's problems as well as releasing trying to solve these problems.

Here is a short mindfulness meditation exercise:

Find a quiet space and a few moments. Sit up comfortably, upright and alert, yet relaxed. Close your eyes or focus your gaze along the line of your nose. Just allow your focus to settle on your breathing. Keep bringing your attention back to your breathing each time your mind wanders – you may find you do this a few hundred times!! Be patient as it is a bit like learning to ride a bicycle – it takes a bit of time and some persistence but it will get easier. This exercise will show you how often and how easy it is for your mind to wander from the present moment and also how possible it is to take control and re direct it. - Lynne Exley

THE POWER OF FOCUS

'The most valuable skill or talent you could ever develop is that of directing your thoughts toward what you want. Focus is not your friend if it is focussing upon conditions that are preventing you from your receptivity' – Esther Hicks

If you have ever watched the professionals being interviewed following a round on television, you will notice a very common theme. At some point the interviewer will question and focus on something that didn't quite go to plan during the round. The response from the player nine times out of ten is to acknowledge what happened, not berate themselves for it, and quite swiftly move on to a positive aspect that happened during the round. They do not allow themselves to harbour on the negative focal point directed by the interviewer. If they did this repetitively throughout the course of a season it would begin to alter their perception of themselves as a golfer, lower their confidence levels and impact their self-belief, not to mention changing the positive neuro-circuitry in their brains.

Have you ever noticed the praise you give yourself after a round of golf or remember listing all of the good shots you hit, not once reminiscing on the bad ones? If you said yes, fantastic! If no, which alas, tends to be the larger majority of golfers then there is work to be done!

Where is our focus?

Many golfers will often focus immediately on the poor shots and what went wrong during the round, all with vivid imagery, a good helping of negative emotion and a dose of negative self-talk. Sometimes this may be played over repeatedly in their mind during the car journey home or to playing partners and fellow golfers in the clubhouse. The more we ingrain these negative thoughts and emotions in our mind and body the more hardwired the negative programme becomes. The greater the limiting beliefs we place upon ourselves, the more our negative perception about ourselves as golfers increases.

Often things begin to spiral in the wrong direction if we are not consciously aware of our negative reactions. The beauty is that where we choose to place our focus is just that, **a choice**. Where there is conscious awareness, there is choice, where there is choice there is an opportunity for change.

Imagine a large, dark warehouse, the lights are switched off and all you have is a flash torch to help you see where things are. For a split second, somebody switches the light on and you notice that in this warehouse are shelves filled with all the fantastic things you could ever imagine or have ever wanted. The light then goes off and you go back to seeing only what your flash torch allows you to. It does not mean those other things are not there it simply means you are not focussed on them. This is exactly the same as our focus both on and off the golf course. It's similar to a common scenario in everyday life where, if you think back to a time when you were buying a car, you decide on one that you like and you then subsequently seem to spot that same model everywhere you go! They were there all along it's just that you weren't focussed on them!

How focus affects our golf

We tend to get what we focus on whether that is wanted or unwanted. Sometimes we are not aware of how much attention (and more importantly, emotion) we put into the things we don't want or as mentioned previously what we fear. That's where our conscious awareness creates an opportunity to selectively step in and choose to redirect us back in the right direction. The only reason this becomes harder in the practical sense is because we have become so used to programming ourselves to look for, or focus on, the negative, that it has become habitual. The mind and body have become conditioned to respond this way.

If you place your primary focus on the shots you feel were poor during the round and berate yourself for these, over a period of time, this will have a hugely detrimental impact on confidence levels. Yes, there may be elements that with some adjustments can be improved upon, but these are to be acknowledged with a positive, solution-orientated approach. The elements of your game that went well must be **your**

first primary focus, rather than playing back in your mind the disaster movies of all that went wrong.

A change in focus

Here is a great exercise to channel your focus: After every round of golf, whether it's a friendly 9 holes or a tournament round, write down at **least three or four things that went well during that round.** It could have been a good course management decision; a well struck 5 iron, anything you felt went well. Keep a little note book in the early stages to help ensure this process remains a repetitive exercise. Once you begin to focus on one positive aspect it is pleasantly surprising how momentum builds and you become much more aware of many other positive points, all of which you were unable to see due to the habitual negative focal point. Eventually, your brain will create new neural pathways and its natural default will be oriented towards a much more positive focal point. This in turn will improve confidence levels and help to change any negative perception you may have of yourself as a golfer. How you perceive yourself as a golfer plays a pivotal role in your performance and levels of success.

Changing your focus may initially be a little battle as the old negative thought patterns will try to take over. However, remember that's just the old programmed habit. I was working with one particular student who was extremely conscientious with regards to wanting to improve her swing and her game. She was however, by her own admission, a perfectionist and very hard on herself. Shots would never quite be good enough, something could always be better and this was generally where she tended to place her focus. Having worked on her swing studiously over the previous 18 months prior to our meeting, she often found herself in a vicious loop, a feeling of a slight improvement but then taking two frustrating steps backwards, unfortunately getting more and more despondent with her game and losing the enjoyment. Following a few sessions together, we went out for 9 holes and I made a mental note of all the positive shots, decisions and outcomes that she made. At the end of the round I asked her to name at least three things she felt went well.

We sat and waited in silence for a while, and then a little while longer, she was stumped and couldn't think of anything as her focus had tended to weigh more heavily on the negative and her natural default was to be a little critical of herself. I had at least half a dozen things lined up in my mind as there had been plenty of positive aspects to choose from. I started to mention a couple and in that instant it triggered her memory, her focus had shifted and she was able to finish the list off for me. From that moment on she kept a notebook and wrote her positive list down after every round, eventually her programmed habit became a positive one and she no longer required the notebook. I saw her a few weeks later, looking like a new woman! With a big smile on her face she explained that she was now enjoying her golf, her handicap dropped by 5 shots in 2 months and in her own words, 'I am no longer looking for the perfect shot, and I love it!!'

Look Ahead, Not Around!

I have to pay tribute to my dad for this little gem of golfing advice! As a youngster, during the years where he would tirelessly caddie for me at various events and tournaments, he would every now and then prompt me with the simple four words, 'Look ahead, not around'. Looking ahead refers to focussing on your **own** game and how you intend to play a particular round/event.

Focussing on your own unique abilities and strengths

The essence of those four words is to focus on your own unique abilities and strengths, rather than on what other people may be doing. When you arrive at the golf course or a tournament, it is essential to feel positive and confident in your own mind that you have prepared to the best of **your** ability and not be deterred by what may be happening around you. That may simply be acknowledging and prioritising that you are there to enjoy your game, accepting you are giving your best efforts in any given moment. Arriving at the golf course or an event and immediately looking around at what other players or competitors are doing in the form of comparison can start to trigger feelings of inferiority and lack or place doubt in your own ability. This has a big impact on confidence levels and self-belief and can have an influence on the round ahead.

You may look around at another player's practice routine and worry that you are not doing things in the same way or doing the same amount of practice as they are prior to your round. You may look at their equipment and feel that yours does not quite match up, or your clubs are not as good as theirs. These subtle (or sometimes not so subtle) perceptions of what is going on around you can start to affect your game even before you head on to the first tee. Comparing yourself to the environment and people around you in a negative light can greatly affect confidence levels, maybe feelings that you are not good enough or talented enough to be playing in or competing at a certain event.

> *The shovel is bigger than the spoon, but it can never ever do the work the spoon does. They both look similar; they both have different sizes but one more thing not to forget is that "they are important in their own roles"! Each is unique! You are unique too. Take the lead!" — Israelmore Ayivor*

The negative impact of looking around and comparing yourself to others rather than looking ahead and focussing inwards on your own abilities and strengths may also continue out on the golf course. If you try to associate, compare or match your own game to your playing partner, it takes you away from your own unique rhythm, timing, strengths and focus. You may try to change your game, perhaps try to drive as far as your playing partner, hit the same iron on a par 3, change your course management strategy or change your swing in some way. Looking around rather than looking ahead can impact things both technically and psychologically. From a technical point of view, very often when trying to match a drive that may have been driven 20 yards beyond our own, we take ourselves away from our own unique timing. If this done in a way that affects the efficiency and sequencing of our own natural motion, it will in fact potentially lose distance and accuracy in the process. Focussing our attention on our own game enables us to swing within ourselves rather than trying to stretch beyond our own unique technique and timing, ultimately producing a more efficient golf swing. It also allows us to make better course management decisions based around our own unique strengths. It encourages a greater sense of inner confidence which brings with it the opportunity to enjoy the round much more. If you notice the feelings that accompany any form of negative comparison to others, it often comes from a sense of lack. This tends to increase tension and anxiety levels and is ultimately not the ideal platform to play our best golf from.

A great tip I had many years ago is to imagine having a loudspeaker sitting on your shoulder. Whatever thoughts you think will project through the loud speaker and be heard by everyone around you! Let's look at a potential example of what this may sound like! You arrive at the club for a tournament or monthly medal and your loud speaker is turned on full with the following:

'Here goes, I never play well in medals or stroke play, gosh that guy has hit balls already and even has time to work on his short game, maybe I should have done that, I feel bad I should have taken time to practice, ah well he's probably much better than me anyway. Hmmm, looks like she has the latest equipment, she must be really good, my old 3 wood will have to do, I'm not good enough to warrant a new

driver anyway. Now then did I turn the iron off/ lock the door when I left?! Right I better have a few putts before teeing off!'

Can you imagine playing your best round of golf after such a self negating onslaught and a mind fraught with worry! You are unique in your own right, play to the rhythm of your own tune, regardless of what is going on around you. Looking around, consumed with what others are doing, takes energy, precious energy that is far better spent embracing and expressing your own unique talents and abilities. Yes we can 'acknowledge' what is going on around us and if we can gain positive insights from our surroundings, great, but the minute it becomes a comparison in a negative sense or becomes a feeling of lack in some way, it is time to change focus and place attention on the unique strengths that lie within. Look ahead, not around!

THE MIND-BODY CONNECTION, WHAT THE SCIENCE SAYS

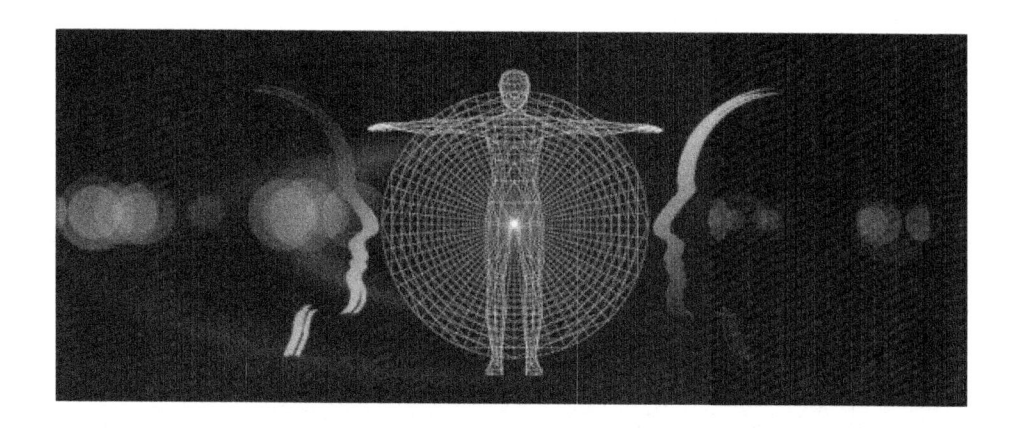

'The mind and the body are like parallel universes. Anything that happens in the mental universe, must leave tracks in the physical one' – **Deepak Chopra**

I understand there are areas within this book, which may have you in a quandary as to which section of the bookstore it was bought from, Sport, Mind Body & Spirit or Science 101! I do very much believe in the importance of the link between these areas in order to maximise potential and enjoyment on the golf course. In this chapter, I will endeavour to explain the evidence behind some of the physiological and scientific references that frequently appear. If you have an inquisitive mind and prefer to know the how's and the whys as to the way things work, you may question how some of the processes I have presented in the past several chapters really work to create a positive effect on your game. Where is the scientific evidence? How does imagery work? How can the way I think and feel really affect any outcome? Some examples have already been offered along the way however this chapter aims to explore things a little further.

Of course, we don't always need to know the complexities of the way certain things work. For example, we just turn the electric switch on and we have light! However if we question or doubt a process that requires our full immersion and belief, it tends to create some resistance and we don't get the results we were hoping for, hence it reinforces our initial disbelief and so the cycle continues. There requires an openness to surrender to the process for you to fully reap the benefits. If this requires logical scientific proof and evidence, then this chapter may hopefully provide some.

With practices such as imagery, focus, breathing and mindfulness, if we are sceptical of their value and simply go through the motions with an internal mantra of 'not really being sure about this mumbo jumbo but will give it a go!' the odds of the desired outcome potentially decreases. For those who require it, scientific evidence can help to satisfy the thirst for logical reasoning behind why or how something works. It provides evidence into how this 'mind stuff' really plays its part! Most importantly, having the evidence may enable you to have a little more faith in the process.

Having said that, I also believe there are times, particularly where the golf swing is concerned, when an overly analytical or logical thought process can be detrimental. From a playing perspective I have to admit to, at times, previously falling into that category within my golfing career. I was a little critical and analytical in terms of the technical aspects of my game and always had to know why/how something happened or worked. This does not contradict in anyway the importance of having a *simplified* understanding of your own swing and game, it is just at times this can be overdone and become an obstacle to progress. From experience both within my competitive years and also within my coaching, I have seen the overly analytical approach and its detrimental effects from both sides of the fence. In constantly fixating on the technical elements of the swing, you can get stuck in a mechanical process leaving little room for trust and flow. Ironically it is trust and flow that can help to create a more technically proficient and efficient movement. Imagine throwing a ball into a basket from a distance. In *constantly* analysing the mechanics of how the arm is getting the ball into the basket with little focus on the basket there becomes an increased chance of missing the desired target!

Throughout the chapters thus far I have detailed the importance of having a basic understanding of your golf swing and its correlation to the ball flight. I am certainly not going against this, however there can be a danger of becoming too heavily focussed on trying to master the technical aspects of your swing and game. This may become a **constant** breakdown of trying to fix several elements of your swing to the point where focus on the target itself has been lost. If you find imagery a difficult process to carry out on the golf course it can often be due to the fact you are less connected to the image as your attention and focus has been placed on the how and why of the golf swing.

I was working with a student who was a highly intellectual gentleman and had qualified as medical professor at a very young age. As a good sportsperson with a background in ice hockey, he very quickly made great strides forward in reducing his handicap and from a starting handicap of 28, steadily came down to the mid-teens. We had some great conversations about the golf swing. He was a student who loved to learn as much as he could about the game and had an extremely competent and in-depth knowledge about the swing relative to the amount of time he had been playing. His ever-inquisitive mind had meant he had studied and taken on board as much knowledge about the game as he could and had enabled him to make good progress. However it started to reach a tipping point where it began to create a roadblock to progressing further. A constant analysis of several areas of the golf swing, particularly following what he felt was a poor hole or round on the course, created the continual experimentation with the vast encyclopaedia of technical knowledge that he had developed. This created a pattern of good days/weeks and bad days/weeks with a struggle to create a long period of consistency. Target-orientated golf with a level of trust in his instinct and natural ability became a more difficult concept to master. Instead, logic and analysis kept getting in the way. Handicap reductions did continue which was great however the roller coaster ride of inconsistencies remained as the search for the logic of the perfect swing and magic answer niggled away at the forefront!

Finding the scientific evidence for improving in golf

Utilising my own degree of rational and logical thinking more productively, I was keen to immerse myself into the world of neuroscience and quantum physics to see how performance in the golfing world, and indeed life itself, could link with the scientific evidence provided. For anybody who feels they favour understanding the scientific proof behind certain concepts, having access to science based evidence can help instil faith in the process.

Evidence: The mind-body connection

Modern day neuroscientists and biologists such as Dr Joe Dispenza and Dr Bruce Lipton are providing scientific research and evidence to back up the mind-body connection and to support the principle that we are in fact the creators of our own lives and not subject to the destiny of our genes, or 'that's just the way I am'!

The field of quantum physics describes the very smallest things in our universe, molecules, atoms, protons, neutrons and electrons. It explores the concept of energy, where everything is made up of atoms simply vibrating at different frequencies. What we see as physical matter are in fact atoms vibrating at a slower frequency. In the quantum physics model atoms act as particles of possibility, experiments have argued the fact that conscious observation has the ability to impact this field of energy and possibility. Dr Joe Dispenza states that thoughts are the electrical charge in the quantum field and feelings are the magnetic charge, how you think and how you feel broadcasts an electromagnetic signature that influences every single atom your life.

> *If you wish to understand the universe, think of energy, frequency and vibration' – Nikola Tesla, Inventor of the radio & wireless communication.*

Imagine a radio station dialled in to 96.2FM. We can't hear what is being played if we are tuned in to 98.6FM, there is interference, it's a different frequency. This is exactly the same with energy. Our thoughts, feelings, beliefs and expectations broadcast an energetic frequency and an exact vibrational match is then mirrored back into our lives. In simple terms you tend to attract into your life the experiences, people and circumstances that reflect your inner world, thoughts, feelings and energy. At this point you might be wondering what on earth this has to do with improving my golf. However bear with me a little longer!

> *'We can no longer consider ourselves merely onlookers who have no effect on the world that we're observing….. The very act of observation is an act of creation' – John Wheeler, American Theoretical Physicist.*

If like attracts like and like energy attracts like energy on a vibration level, then whatever you focus on will grow whether that is wanted or unwanted. If we are on the golf course focussing on fear or anxiety, whether that be fear of hitting a shot in the water or fear of finishing last in the tournament we are summoning like thoughts, feelings, energy and ultimately drawing that outcome closer into our experience. Because like energy/emotions attract like energy/emotions, once you begin to think a negative thought, other similar negative thoughts and emotions are attracted and build in momentum. Remember, too, that the body's chemical **thinking and feeling loop**, discussed previously, feed this process. Of course on the flip side of this is the opportunity to attract and build on positive and expansive thoughts, feelings and emotions.

Let's look at another example: You know sometimes in the morning, you wake up, and as the saying goes 'on the wrong side of the bed'. You're grumpy, it's raining outside and you trip over the shoe left from the night before on the way to the bathroom! You burn the toast in the toaster, get in the car to work, all the lights turn red as you pull up to them and every road user in your vicinity seems to have lost all road manners, cutting you up at every opportunity. And so it continues, it spirals into a series of frustrating events, one after the other. What might happen if you could rewind the events of the day to that minute your head lifted the pillow and made a conscious decision that nothing is more important than that you feel good? What if at that moment, you decided what kind of a day you want to have? Perhaps as you opened the curtains you were undeterred by and in fact appreciating that it was raining, the garden would flourish as a result and it was well in need of a downpour! It is likely that a whole set of different circumstances and trail of events would ensue. This is because you are in a very different emotional state and transmitting a different frequency and energy.

Think back to a time on the golf course where a snowball of events has happened one after another. You three putt the first green and feeling slightly anxious, you then recall that in your last round you had done the same thing. This reminded you how things go downhill if you start off a bit shaky, which leads you to remembering how you have been struggling with your putting. Feeling a bit tense you tweak your next tee shot into the trees on the right of the fairway. You are frustrated with yourself as you remind yourself you always land there on that hole and how it normally ends up being a disaster hole! Perhaps this leads to a new thought: 'I'm going to finish last at this rate unless something drastically improves!' or 'That's it, it's going to be one of those days!' After just the first two holes you have managed to spiral into a fear of finishing at the end of the field or a resignation to 'one of those days!'! This is how quickly our mind can runaway with us.

The beauty, however, is that **if we can create an anxious spiral of the unwanted, we can absolutely do the opposite, the minute we make the decision and gain the awareness.**

> *'When you begin to understand Law of Attraction, and you understand that which is like unto itself is drawn, then it is easier and easier to understand that you are offering a signal, and the entire Universe responds. And when you finally get that,*

and you begin to exercise some deliberate control about the signal that you offer, then it really begins to be fun, because then you recognize that nothing happens outside of your creative control. There are no things that happen by chance or by circumstance. There is nothing that is happening because of something you vibrated a long time ago. It is not about what you were born into. It is only about what you are, right now, in this red hot fresh moment emitting.' - Esther Hicks

Mental Rehearsal

Mental rehearsal has also been well-documented within the sporting field, including the value of creating a clear intention in your mind and attaching positive emotion prior to the event. So how does this really work? Research has shown that physiological, change can occur purely through the mental image. A study was undertaken at Harvard University in the USA into research subjects who had never played the piano before. The research subjects **mentally** practised a simple, five finger piano exercise for two hours a day for five days. A second group of research subjects **physically** practised the same simple piano activities. The findings showed that the group who only practiced the piano exercises mentally made the same changes in the brain as the subjects who physically practised the same activities, but without ever lifting a finger.

> *'The region of their brains that controls the finger movements increased dramatically, allowing their brains to look as though the experience they'd imagined had actually happened. They installed the neurological circuits and programs, thereby creating new brain maps. If you keep placing your awareness in the same place, you are firing and wiring the same networks of neurons, as a result you build stronger brain maps in that area.'*
> - Dr Joe Dispenza

Dr. Dennis Waitley trained astronauts and Olympic athletes to use visualisation processes to achieve success.

> *'I took the visualization process from the Apollo program and instituted it during the 1980s and '90s into the Olympic program. And it was called Visual Motor Rehearsal. When you visualize, then you materialize. And the interesting thing about the mind is, we took Olympic athletes and then hooked them up to sophisticated biofeedback equipment, and had them run their event ONLY in their mind. Incredibly, the same muscles fired, in the same sequence when they were running the race in their mind, as when they were running it on the track. How could this be? Because the mind can't distinguish whether you're really doing it, or whether it's just a practice. I think if you've been there in the mind, you'll go there in the body.'* - Dennis Waitley

When we begin to create a new image, thought and emotion in our mind, the body begins to change neurologically and chemically. There are also many documented cases of people who have healed their body of illness through a change in emotions, and in turn their internal chemistry, through thoughts, beliefs and imagery. Their body responded to a new internal chemistry and neurocircuitry. The scientific concepts go into far greater detail and this is only really touching the surface. However, the key here is simply to provide an acknowledgement of the scientific research and evidence that confirms and backs up how significantly the mind and body are connected. If we approach the game of golf thinking that the two are not intrinsically linked I believe we are missing out on a huge link to successful performance.

Science, evidence and golf

If having an understanding of the information that science is providing allows us to make changes for the better and trust in the process, then it is has done its job well. If we understand the principles of universal energy, the laws of attraction and inclusion, we know that an internal emotional mix of anxiety, fear and unworthiness is unlikely to produce the positive outcomes we desire, whether that is approaching a tee shot down the last hole of a tournament or any other situation in life. If we can dissolve the negative momentum, and utilise the power of choice to focus on the positive aspects, our wants and our desires, then we are in the driving seat and possibilities become limitless.

Science backs the notion that not only can the physical body be healed, influenced and changed through our thoughts, emotions and energy but also our external environment around us, and that we are in fact, powerful creators of our reality.

PERCEPTION – THE FILTERS OF SUCCESS

'If you change the way you look at things, the things you look at change' – *Wayne Dyer*

How is it that two people can walk away from a party telling two very different stories of their experience, or how two people arrive at a golf tournament, one person is full of excitement and adrenaline, the other is full of dread and anxiety - exactly the same external event yet very different internal states? How we perceive a situation gives us a different outlook, different feelings and in turn, behaviours regarding a particular event or situation. A person's perception (or perceived reality of a situation) will be influenced by the brain's ability to internally process the information received. Due to the high volume of information the conscious mind receives moment by moment, to cope with the heavy load it is internally processed and is either: *deleted*, *distorted* or *generalised*.

> *Deleted:* **Selectively paying attention to certain aspects of a situation and not others**
>
> *Distorted:* **Making misrepresentations of reality**
>
> *Generalised:* **When a specific experience then represents a whole class of experiences**

The brain filters information and causes any of the above three things to happen. These filters are based around our memories, beliefs, values, experiences and attitudes that have developed over the years. Because each person's filters will be very different, the same information going in will be filtered differently creating a different perception of the same external event. This then becomes their perceived reality.

Let's put these filters this into context. Your ball lies behind a 30ft oak tree. You have a good score card in your hand and only a few holes left to play. How you perceive this situation can be crucial. Do you perceive this as the end of the road - 'Just my bad luck, the wheels had to come off at some point'? Or do you perceive it with a degree of excitement - 'I love a challenge, how can I use my creative skills here?' These two different perceptions of the same situation will quite likely produce very different results. What is your perception of a certain situation on the golf course and most importantly - **how does**

it influence not only the shot in hand but also your game beyond that point?.

How do you perceive a competitive situation? Do you relish the challenge and feel excitement or do you feel fear, anxiety or dread? How do you perceive yourself as a golfer? Do you see yourself as skilled, competent and consistent, or do you feel inferior to your desired handicap, your aspirations or other players?

How do you perceive a challenging shot on the golf course? Do you think, 'how can I use my creative skills' or 'Oh no, it's the end of the road for me, bang goes my good score card?!'

Once you become aware of your thought process and how you perceive a situation, and the awareness really is the initial key, if the automatic default is in some way negative or it's not serving you in some way, it's an opportunity for change. Ask the question, how can I view this situation differently? Begin to break any old patterns and create a window of choice to perceive them in a way that is more beneficial and moves you closer to your desired outcome.

How you perceive yourself as a golfer is hugely important and greatly influences your golfing behaviour. Let's take the example of newcomers to the game who have been playing for a little while, have gained competency and improved, yet still perceive themselves as beginners. You often hear it in the language that they use when describing themselves, such as, 'Oh I'm just a beginner, put me at the end of the field in the competition' or 'I'm not good enough to play in competitions.' They hold on to the perception of being a beginner and in doing so create a road block for moving beyond that point and fulfilling their true potential. It can, at times, almost act as a safety net. It applies not only to beginners but any level of golfer who places limitations on their capabilities and are resistant to allowing themselves to perceive their skill set outside of their current ability or expand beyond the confines of their perceived boundaries. Once you can begin to imagine, believe, perceive and feel you are moving beyond any boundaries or limitations you may have placed on yourself it becomes possible for it to take shape in physical form.

> *'Our deepest fear is not that we are inadequate. Our deepest fear is that we are powerful beyond measure. It is our light, not our darkness that most frightens us. We ask ourselves, who am I to be brilliant, gorgeous, talented, fabulous? Actually, who are you* **not** *to be? Your playing small does not serve the world. As we let our own light shine, we unconsciously give other people permission to do the same'* – Marianne Williamson

With a little reflection, if you can become consciously aware of, acknowledge, and begin to positively change any limiting or negative perceptions you have of either yourself as a golfer or any situations you may find yourself in on the golf course, you will reap the benefits both in results and enjoyment. Awareness to a pattern of thought and perception that doesn't serve you is the first stepping stone. From here changes can begin to be made. Remember it is only your perceived reality, any pattern of thought that feels restrictive and one that is holding you back from your true potential in some way, in simple terms, just won't 'feel' good. This becomes the opportunity to shift things in a way that serves and supports you and moves you closer to your desired outcome and goals. A different internal response and perception can in turn influence a very different outcome.

> *'Between stimulus and response there is a space. In that space is our power to choose our response. In our response lies our growth and our freedom'* – *Viktor Frankl*

THE PITFALLS OF A PERFECTIONIST

'Perfectionism is the 20 tonne shield that we lug around thinking it will protect us when, in fact it's the thing that's really preventing us from being seen and taking flight' – Brene Brown

Herein lays the question: are there beneficial gains to being a perfectionist? During my early years of competition I certainly believed so. I truly thought that if I put exceedingly high expectations on myself with very little room for error, and gave myself a bit of a hard time for performing below what I thought was possible, I would push myself to achieving more. If I could turn back the hands of time I would certainly change my perspective on that one! On reflection it did nothing more than create tension, frustration and an obstacle to achieving my goals, not to mention taking the fun and enjoyment out of the whole process.

Typically a perfectionist can often fall into the trap of focussing on what needs to be fixed, perceived flaws, what could be better or what went wrong. Certainly positives are gained from being intrinsically driven and wanting to achieve the best from oneself, however, when based primarily around self criticism and judgement with little support or reflection and acknowledgement of the positives, progress and enjoyment can be thwarted. It tends to create a never ending loop of toil, hardship and tension with very little time, if any, to enjoy the fruits of ones labour. From a coaching perspective I have often worked with students who have strived and successfully achieved in many areas of their lives either in other sports, careers etc, and they then give themselves a particularly hard time and feel extremely frustrated if they find the road to golfing success a little bumpier. Unfortunately where golf is concerned the more you berate yourself for things not going to plan, the harder you try, the greater the tension develops and the worse it gets! The perfectionist hits, by his or her standards, a poor shot, and so the analysis begins, 'what happened in my swing, what do I need to fix?', 'I can't believe I did that, I know I can hit that shot so much better.' From here the downward spiral potentially continues.

This may raise the question, 'How can I get the best from myself if I don't push to extremes and expect the very highest of standards?' It doesn't mean that having a sloppy approach to things or setting low standards is the alternative option. It simply means that if we constantly give ourselves a hard time about what went wrong or what needs fixing without room to acknowledge the positives or see the areas to improve as simply an opportunity to grow it creates a build up of frustration, tension and potentially a less enjoyable path to our desired destination. From here it can only unfortunately lead to a negative spiral on the golf course, physical tension will impact the golf swing and we will generally not always make the best decisions tactically from this state of mind either. Being aware of, and acknowledging your strengths and seeing perceived weaknesses as merely areas for growth will provide a much more fruitful experience and end result, leading to increased confidence and enjoyment of your game. Golfers who give themselves an extremely hard time and who, when they reach a certain goal, spend very little time, if any, acknowledging or praising their achievements, simply plough more energy into achieving more and more, ultimately neglecting the one reason they took up the game, to have fun and for the enjoyment of it!

'It makes no difference how many peaks you reach, if you did not enjoy the climb' – Oprah Winfrey

Acknowledging your strengths with praise creates confidence. Acknowledging areas that need development, with encouragement and support, also assists in alleviating tension and provides a positive progression forward. Continually berating yourself for your perceived flaws does not. Getting the best from yourself comes from a state of ease, self-confidence, belief and enjoyment in the process. The more we focus on the enjoyment of the process whilst embracing the opportunity to grow versus the fear of making a mistake or falling short of expectations, the greater the opportunity of fulfilling our potential. The good shots feel effortless; they are rarely a result of tension, effort or hardship. Be easy on yourself and remember, as simple as it sounds, the better you feel, the better it gets!

> *'Spend more time smiling than frowning and more time praising than criticising!' – Richard Branson*

How mind-set affects success

In her work on motivation, achievement and success, the American psychologist, Carol Dweck, researched and developed the 'fixed mindset' v the 'growth mindset' concept. People with a fixed mindset believe that their intelligence is fixed. They base any activities that they carry out on whether their intelligence will be shown at an advantage. They will base it on whether they will 'feel smart'.

People with a growth mind-set believe in change, growth and the opportunity in learning from their mistakes without being hard on themselves. They are curious about life, what it has to offer and what can be learnt. They believe that intellectual ability or intelligence can be developed with passion, study and education.

Dweck carried out an experiment where 400 children were split into two groups and given various tests and puzzles to carry out. At the end of the tests the two groups were given praise. One group's praise was relayed to them as 'you were good at that.' The other group received praise, worded slightly differently as 'you made a good effort'. In short the second group were praised on their levels of effort rather than their intelligence. Interestingly, when the groups went on to do further tests, Dweck found that the **group praised for being good at something** chose the easier options (they wanted to remain in the boundaries of their perceived intelligence and wanted to remain 'looking smart'). The **group who received praised based on their effort** went on to complete and succeed in much more difficult tests.

Dweck continued her research by providing an 8-week course for another two groups of students. One group were taught their studies in the usual way. The other group were taught their studies but in addition were also taught the principles of a growth mind-set. This second group were frequently taught that the brain is like a muscle that can continue to grow. New brain connections can be developed over time and taught to believe in the growth of new skills. Importantly they were also taught that 'nobody laughs at babies.' In other words, it's ok to admit to mistakes and to believe that they can be overcome. Dweck found that the students who were taught using the growth mind-set made significant improvement in their grades by the end of the experiment.

The fixed mindset generally places very little room for error with regards to their performance and any mistakes that are made are taken extremely personally with a 'must try harder' attitude. There is a fear of being judged and not being good enough. Embracing the principles of a growth mindset, an approach that acknowledges mistakes and believes they can be overcome, learns from errors and overcomes challenges rather than avoiding them. Striving to achieve for their own intrinsic drive tends to allow them to achieve more, be happier and feel inspired.

Adopting a growth mindset

1. **Learn to hear the voice of the fixed mindset**

'I'm normally good at any sport I take up, I knew it was a risk taking up golf, people will laugh at me thinking I had talent, If I fail partly it is as bad as being a complete failure, people will think bad of me if I make a mistake.'

2. **Recognise that you have a choice in how you interpret what you perceive as setbacks**

3. **Talk back to it with a supportive and growth mindset voice.**

'I'm really enjoying learning a new skill and looking forward to developing as I go along, there's plenty of professional guidance out there to help me on my way as and when I need a little help. It's going to be fun, I'm glad I've embraced the opportunity and looking forward to the challenge!'

Dweck's research findings demonstrated that students who were taught using the principle of a growth mind-set is strongly linked to optimal performance whether that be in the classroom, board room or golf course! Release the chains of perfectionism and most importantly, be easy on yourself!

You are not your golf score; you are way more than that!

It is also important to remember that your performance and results do not define who you are as a person, the moment the two become intertwined it can feel like a 10 tonne weight piles on your shoulders and can create a road block to reaching your potential.

Having an inner confidence and belief in your ability within a specific skill or sport is of course important to fulfilling and maximising your goals and optimising performance. However, defining your self-worth from the outcome of your performance, or in this specific context, golf score, is a very different matter. It is vital to differentiate the two.

> *'Trust in your preparation. You have done all you can, so focus on that fact. You will remain the same person before, during and after the race, so the result, however important, will not define you'* - Chrissie Wellington, 13 times World Ironman Triathlete

It is important to nurture an inner confidence, **an unconditional acceptance of self, regardless of any outcome, goals or**

expectations that you feel may have been placed on you. If self-confidence and self-acceptance rely heavily on your performance on the golf course or your golf score, a great deal of additional pressure is felt to achieve that outcome. This pressure can lead to tension and self criticism, ultimately inhibiting the natural flow and ability of any golfer. It can bring with it that gnawing feeling of not quite being able to reach the potential you know you are capable of.

Embracing self acceptance and nurturing an inner confidence without it ever being linked to any endeavour, result or outcome, is top of the priority list. You are so much more than the results on your score card or performance on the golf course, regardless of how many fairways you hit, putts you hole or shots you take.

> *'We don't realise that we are actually perfect just the way we are. We are born perfect, but spend a lifetime trying to be something we are not, and then feel inadequate for failing. Your only purpose is to be yourself; otherwise you will deprive the universe of who you came here to be. You are loved unconditionally, for no other reason than simply because you exist'* – *Anita Moorjani*

Nurturing inner self-confidence

When you create, develop and nurture inner confidence and acceptance from within, regardless of external circumstances, your true ability will begin to shine. Separating and acknowledging your true essence as a human being and allowing your self-worth to remain fully intact and untouched by the end result, will enable you to fulfil your true potential and without doubt enjoy your golf every time you go out to play, which is ultimately the most important aim of the game! The necessity of becoming your own best friend rather than worst enemy or critic is paramount. You will always be able to tell which one is in control at any one time, the inner critic will create feelings of tension and anxiety. Unconditional self love, regardless of the external conditions, will create feelings of ease, not to mention a resistance free physiology, ultimately allowing you to produce a more free flowing golf swing that is a much closer match to your natural ability.

Self criticism may have become the natural default position over the years hence change can require becoming a conscious observer and catching ourselves in the act when it happens. The self critic will often attach themselves to a specific behaviour, i.e. **I am** foolish, **I am** hopeless, this can have a big impact on confidence levels. Feel the difference between 'that was a foolish thing to do' and 'I am foolish'. Of course ideally a more positive reframe and focus would be more beneficial however there is still a different emotional charge and energy between the two. The first statement of 'that was a foolish thing to do' offers a form of detachment which generally feels a little lighter. The second statement of 'I am foolish' implies a personal attack on character and feels a great deal heavier in comparison.

On the golf course there is a very different energy and feeling both emotionally and within our physiology between criticism/judgement and self love/support.

Let's take the example of the tee shot that goes out of bounds on the first tee.

'I cannot believe I just did that, what a fool I am, I always let myself down in these situations. It's going to be one of my usual hopeless rounds' – Criticism/judgement

Feel the difference in energy between a response filled with criticism/judgement versus one based around self love and support.

'It's ok, there's plenty of time, and it's the first shot of the day. I put a reasonably good swing on the ball considering I didn't get the chance to warm up as much as I would have liked, all is well, I'm looking forward to an enjoyable day.' Support/self love

The above statements and the difference in their emotional charge will greatly affect the success of the following shot and shots thereafter not least due to the change in tension based physiology.

Feeding and nourishing your inner confidence and self worth allows you to accept the outcome knowing it does not change who you are as a person. Playing from this place of knowing allows you step out of the way and allows your natural ability the opportunity to shine through. The ability you knew deep down was there all along.

You are far more than your golf game, so whether you shoot 60, 70, 80, 90 or 100+, in the words of Chrissie Wellington, **'The results, however important, will not define you!'**

TRUST

'If you don't trust yourself, you'll only trust your swing when it's working perfectly' – *Dr Bob Rotella*

Trust begins to play a vital role within our performance, trust not only in the context of our game and our ability but also in the context of ourselves in a generic sense. Trust in self can play a huge part in terms of performance and importantly, in life in general. It can certainly become a determining factor in several different scenarios on the golf course. This was something I could very much resonate with during my earlier years of playing and competing. On reflection, at the time, I lacked an internal trust in my own abilities as a whole and as a result focused heavily on perfecting the technical elements of the golf swing. It felt a more reliable source to trust. On the days where I felt my game was a little 'off track' I didn't feel I had anything to fall back on and things could deteriorate quite quickly. I was always taken aback when playing with or competing against a fellow competitor and being intrigued as to what they were working on in their swing technically and their response being 'nothing!' I used to find it fascinating as I was always bound up in perfecting a certain movement or position. This certainly became a detrimental factor within my game and I think it was the technical fascination that led me into the world of coaching, of which I certainly have no regrets! Having trust in self not just within a golfing context, is so important to all levels of golfer and for sure was a missing factor for me personally and one that would have been a huge road block towards a successful career competing professionally had the opportunity arisen.

Let's look at the role trust plays in different situations within the context of our golf game. Firstly looking at the all too common scenario of our performance on the driving range versus the golf course, how it can differ and in particular when working on a swing change or any change within our game following professional guidance or a coaching session. There are many times when working on a new movement can feel a little different during the initial stages, which is natural when the body has been used to doing something in a certain way for a period of time. When making these changes on the practice ground/driving range the benefits may be two-fold. Firstly being able to build in some form of repetition enables greater opportunity of developing the new feeling/movement replacing the old habits and pattern of movement. The second factor brings the trust element into play. In a practice scenario where we have a volume of balls to get through and we have several attempts in an environment where there isn't any perceived consequence to the result of the shot, we will trust a new feeling much more. On the golf course where we only have one attempt each time and we potentially attach a consequence to the result, as much as intellectually we know the ideal movement or feeling we have been working on we still want to trust and hang on to the old movement/feeling, it almost becomes a bit of a safety blanket. This is one of the reasons why, when developing your game, things may feel positive on the driving range or short game area and yet when transitioning on to the course it can feel a little more hit and miss. There can be times where we may feel in between the old and the new, as with many patterns of habit, it can feel tough initially to trust the new fully and let go of the old, particularly in an environment where we may feel under a little more pressure, i.e. in a tournament or event. Ideally, if we can begin to develop some form of trust in the new feeling initially through repetition in an environment where we perceive there to be little consequence to the result of the outcome and can relax into the process such as the driving range, it creates a greater opportunity of a smoother transition and a level of trust on the golf course.

Trust on the golf course can also begin to make an impact on our performance from a technical perspective. When trust is limited, either in ours elves, our ability or golf swing, there are often times where, from a technical view point, it can begin to suffer. This is primarily due to tension and feeling the need to control the movement and the outcome. So how does this specifically transpire? In relation to the golf swing, it often feels safer to keep the bigger muscles, i.e. the upper body, thorax and shoulders closer to or over the ball, rather than allowing the body to effectively and efficient rotate both during the back swing, through swing and post impact. Tension builds and the movement relies either on the smaller muscles, i.e. the hands and arms to do the work which when used in isolation of a relaxed and efficient body motion can affect both distance and accuracy, or the body will move in a more lateral or vertical motion. All of the above create a feeling of remaining safer and more in control by staying over the ball rather than allowing the body to create an efficient rotary motion. A more rotary motion, which in effect generates the feeling of turning away from the ball and target during the backswing and freely turning towards the target during and post impact won't feel as comfortable to do if trust is lacking in ourselves or golf swing. One of the biggest links between the physiology of trust and the golf swing lies in the degree of tension. In trying to excessively control the golf club or the outcome there lies a greater chance of producing a less technically efficient movement and potentially creating more of the shot we are trying to avoid. Trusting, letting go and releasing excessive tension moves us closer to the desired result.

The role of imagery has been discussed in greater detail in a previous chapter however it is worth highlighting that creating a clear visual of the shot we are aiming to produce can also provide a positive platform where trust is concerned. It creates a clear focal point and reduces the potential of internal negative chatter, shifting the focus of what could go wrong to what we are aiming to achieve. This allows a greater opportunity of trusting the process. It also allows our natural instinct and ability to respond to and reproduce the positive visual.

Another effective approach is once the club choice has been made, target chosen and shot confirmed, simply from that point play the shot with the perspective that it really doesn't matter where the ball goes beyond that point. It can feel quite a liberating experience and pleasantly surprising how easy it feels, letting go can provide a great feeling of relief and in turn creates the opportunity to produce the positive results we were after all along. This is often the mindset we have on the range that allows us to trust the process a little more. Golf can often be played from a place of control, either trying to excessively control the golf club or the outcome of the result. The more this can be replaced with a feeling of letting go and trusting of both the self and the process the more enjoyable the game becomes and the greater chance of the outcome more closely matching our desired results. Very often as simple as it sounds, physical tension will provide the feedback and gauge as to whether we are trying to control the outcome or whether we are placing trust in both ourselves and the process.

'Self Trust is the first secret of success' – *Ralph Waldo Emerson*

GUIDING THE YOUNG GOLFER

'I think one of the things that we need to learn and teach our children is that it is not important to compare ourselves to others, or compete or pursue. All we have to do is be ourselves. Discover who you are and express who you are with abandon' – Anita Moorjani.

Through the years of coaching children, I often have witnessed how confidently they will step up to a 20ft putt for example, free from doubt and trusting their natural instinct to roll it into their intended target. Young children generally place very few limitations on what they believe is possible. It is sometimes through the conditioning of society that layers of limitation can potentially start to build. It is only as we get older do we start to question or doubt, increasing our fears and patterns of limiting beliefs.

> *'Children are happy because they don't have a file in their minds called - 'all the things that could go wrong'* – Marianne Williamson

I remember vividly the day I was coaching a young 7-year-old girl. Following my conversation with her in the English language, she then turned around to her Swedish mother, spoke fluently in her mother tongue and then proceeded to tell me she also spoke a 3rd language owing to her father's Dutch side of the family! This little girl had simply taken on board what was around her; it was natural to her to speak several languages! She had yet to develop any beliefs or limitations about languages being a challenge to learn or that understanding more than two languages was a really difficult feat, especially for a young child. Unlimited potential lies in every human being of all ages, it is only through adding the layers of limiting beliefs and conditioning that we lose sight of what is possible.

Over three hundred years ago, Burma planned to invade Thailand, then known as Siam. The Siamese monks were in possession of a most amazing Buddha statue; made of solid gold it stood over 10 feet tall and weighed over 2 tons. The monks were determined to protect the precious Buddha that meant so much to them so they covered him with clay 12 inches thick believing, rightly, the invading soldiers would ignore it, thinking it was of little value. Sadly, all the monks who were aware of the true identity of the Buddha were killed in the invasion and the secret stayed hidden from the world for two centuries.

In the mid 1950's, the monastery housing the Buddha was to be relocated and the unsuspecting monks arranged for a crane to move the 'clay' Buddha to its new location. However, when the crane started to lift the statue, it was much heavier than expected and began to crack. Mystified the monks lowered it back to the ground and decided to wait until the next day to bring in a more powerful crane. To add insult to injury, it started to rain so the monks covered the statue with tarpaulins to keep it dry. During the night, the head monk went out to make sure the Buddha was adequately covered, shining his torch across the statue. When the light of torch shone into a crack in the clay, he saw a glimmer, a reflection of something underneath the clay. He immediately started to carefully chisel away shards of clay to find that the glimmer grew brighter. Hours later, when all the clay had been removed he found himself in the presence of a Buddha made of solid gold. It now resides in The Temple of the Golden Buddha in Bangkok, Thailand.

This is how we all start out, shining brightly as did the Golden Buddha, unfortunately sometimes the layers of mud develop as limiting beliefs are impressed upon us, often from the external environment. The good news is the Golden Buddha is always there and never leaves!

What does it mean for the young golfer?

As mentioned previously in an earlier chapter, the brain waves of a young child up until the age of 7 operate at a slower almost trance like state of Theta, hence they are very receptive to the influences around them. They are like little sponges. As a teacher or parent it is extremely important to be conscious of what influences, thoughts and beliefs are being created around them.

> *'Young Children carefully observe their environment and download the worldly wisdom offered by parents directly into their subconscious memory. As a result, their parents' behaviour and beliefs become their own'* – Dr Bruce Lipton

Children want to have fun and for them, and in fact everyone, golf should be fun. However, children are prone to feeling the pressures of the people and loved ones around them. They want so much to fulfil their parents' expectations and hopes. I have often witnessed where this transforms into tension and disappointment as the child places pressure on themselves if they don't feel they have succeeded in certain tasks. Tears have flowed when they have been the first one to drop the bean bag in a fun warm up game or they missed the final putt to pass their bronze certificate.

It can also stretch into young adulthood. Governing sporting bodies and coaches who take the reins as the child progresses can be a huge influence and it is extremely important for it to be a positive one. If a child or young adults perception of their self-worth is measured in whether they make the National squad, shoots a certain score or qualifies for the tour, the pressure that puts on them will potentially cause a detrimental impact at some point, even to the point where interest in the game begins to weaken and an alternative takes centre stage as a replacement.

A supportive role where they know they are loved regardless of the outcome is the very best platform we can create to allow children to develop, enjoy and fulfil their goals and dreams. I truly believe that within sport and within life itself, if we can provide children with an unconditional love, support and acceptance that no matter what score they achieve on the golf course, whether they gain their red certificate in their junior coaching class or shoot a sub-par score in an elite junior event, they are loved for the fantastic human being that they are. When they know this to their core they will truly excel. It is the pressure of seeking love, acceptance and approval from the people that mean so much to them that can place the tension and resistance into their progress.

It's about having fun

Ultimately it's about having fun, whatever the age! This certainly doesn't mean there isn't a place for dedication, goals and focus, however when the young golfer is encouraged from a place of self-love, worth and belief, regardless of the outcome, fantastic results in the long term potentially transpire and certainly with a great deal more enjoyment in the process.

Based on psychological research, the 3 healthiest statements parents can make as they perform are:

Before the competition:

    1. Have fun.

    2. Play hard.

    3. I love you.

After the competition:

    1. Did you have fun?

    2. I'm proud of you.

    3. I love you.

Following decades of research long time coaches Bruce Brown and Rob Miller from Proactive coaching concluded that there are six simple words parents can express that produce the most productive results. When college athletes were asked what their parents said that made them feel great, that amplified their joy during and after a ballgame. Their overwhelming response:

'I love to watch you play'

Unconditional love and support, free from judgement regardless of the outcome, creates an environment that allows each child to thrive and develop whilst embracing the ultimate goal of having fun.

EPILOGUE

Golf is a fantastic game to be enjoyed both as a physical pursuit and also I believe, as a great teacher of life. Over the years I have found through both my own playing experiences and the pleasure of meeting a wealth of different students with their own individual personalities, character and uniqueness, that there are so many traits about both ourselves as human beings and everyday life that we can learn and develop on the golf course. Golf encourages us to understand the importance of self belief, patience, focus, self worth and mindfulness, to trust in our own inbuilt innate wisdom and capabilities. Not to listen to the negative chatter box within which can often be the voices of either others people's perceptions or our misperceptions of reality. So many different qualities can be gained and embraced in this great game.

> *'Golf is the loneliest sport. You're completely alone with every conceivable opportunity to defeat yourself. Golf brings out your assets and liabilities as a person. The longer you play the more certain you are that a man's performance is the outward manifestation of who, in his heart, he really thinks he is.' - Hale Irwin*

So is there really a magic answer to the never-ending search of golfing mastery? I don't believe the magic answer lies in one particular movement, i.e. keeping the head down, the left arm straight or a perfect leading wrist at impact. This is not to say these are incorrect in some shape or form during the swing, however the continual search for that one bit of magic in a standalone solitary movement may become a long frustrating process. In summary, I do believe some of the answers lie in a solid starting position and basic fundamentals of the set up, a solid short game, a simple conceptual and self-empowered understanding of the golf swing, and the final pillar to support these key areas and where I believe the real magic lies is ultimately within. Your thoughts, emotions and beliefs have the potential to hold the true magic! The longer the search remains **solely** on the external whether that is through the latest driver, putter or swing theory, the longer the magic answer will continue to remain elusive or at least inconsistently so. There may be a glimmer of euphoria now and then and there is certainly no denying that in their own right they can aid progression, however long term consistency becomes a much greater task. Can degrees of data provided by the latest radar technology when professionally interpreted provide progress to the elite and club golfer? Yes. Can technical improvements, whether that is locating optimal ball position on the putting green or solid postural positions in the set-up assist golfers progression? Absolutely. Can a golf fit body potentially outperform its counterpart? Definitely. They all provide pieces to the bigger whole. I do believe however, that the glue that bonds the success of these components together and that which provides consistency on a long term basis, resides within.

The notion that golf is based around addressing a static ball rather than reacting to a moving ball like many other ball sports creates a slightly more unique momentary space to either trust and allow our own natural abilities to shine through or to create a doorway for self doubt, negative chatter and fear. If the latter, it simply provides a great window of opportunity and learning curve of how we can develop and grow both to improve our games and ourselves as human beings in everyday life; either way a win win! It is my wish that the enclosed chapters have assisted in some way or at least shone some light on how we may keep developing on that learning curve. Enjoy the process, the journey and everything this great game has to offer!

End Notes

Sloping Lies Bullet Points

The below are based around a right handed golfer. Each golfer's natural ball flight will also come into play with regards to the direction of the shot however the standard ball flight in accordance with the relevant slope are included. Where possible create a balanced starting position and prioritise maintaining balance as much as possible throughout the shot. This may at times, depending on the severity of the shot, mean swinging to around 70-80% of your full capacity. Ideally always feel as though you are working with the slope rather than against it. Where possible aim to link any similarities present between the various slopes to help with simplifying the process and deepening the understanding.

Ball Above your feet:

Ball Flight Tendency: Will travel left in the air

When the ball is above the feet the hands and arms tend to become more active and encourage the club to be swung on more of an arc. The flatter motion combined with active hands creates a fuller release, a closing down of the clubface through impact and the tendency for the ball to travel left in the air. The slope will also change the way the club sits on the ground during the set up and will encourage the loft of the club to aim to the left, another contributing factor to the ball travelling to the left.

Aim: Aim the leading edge of the clubface to the right of target, the amount dependent on the severity of the slope. The feet, knees, hips and shoulders will be parallel to this target line.

Grip: Grip down the handle due to the ball being closer to you. This will increase control and ensure the slope does not get in the way of the club.

Ball Position: Central in the stance - The club is now swung on more of an arc, the centre of the stance is where the club is on line with the target.

Stance/posture: As normal. Posture may feel a little more upright, depending on the severity of the slope, optimising balance is key.

Swing: Swing in balance

Ball below your feet

Ball flight Tendency: Will travel right in the air

The priority here is to maintain balance and posture angles (created in the set up) throughout the shot as much as possible, avoiding the temptation to pull up. When maintaining a slightly more squatted posture, the body becomes less mobile and the hands and arms work more independently, the club is generally swung a little more upright with less clubface rotation through impact. This has the tendency to cause the ball to travel to the right, hence the ball more often than not will finish right of the target unless corrections are made with the alignment in the set up. The slope will also change the way the club sits on the ground during the set up and will encourage the loft of the club to aim to the right, another cause of ball potentially travelling to right in the air. An additional club i.e. 6 iron rather than 7 iron may be required due to any spin imparted on the ball potentially reducing the distance of the shot.

Aim: Aim the leading edge of the club face to the left of target, the amount dependant on the severity of the slope. The feet, hips and shoulders will be parallel to this target line.

Grip: Hold the club at its full length due to the ball being further away in the set up.

Ball position: As normal

Stance/posture: To create stability and maintain balance add a little extra knee flex in the posture if required where the slope is particularly severe.

Swing: Maintain posture and knee flex throughout the shot, avoid pulling up through impact.

Uphill Lie

Ball Flight: Will travel left in the air & higher trajectory

When faced with an uphill lie the slope will add extra loft to the club through impact resulting in a shot that will fly a little higher than normal, the amount depending on the severity of the slope. The lower body also becomes more restricted through impact due to the weight and body hanging back and favouring the lower foot whilst it marries up with the slope. It becomes more difficult to transfer weight; hence the club is more likely to pass the hands at impact causing the clubface to close down and the ball to travel to the left.

Aim: Aim the leading edge of the clubface to the right of target, the amount dependent on the severity of the slope. The feet, knees, hips and shoulders will be parallel to this target line.

Grip: As normal. If the slope is particularly severe hold further down the handle to avoid the slope getting in the way through impact and to encourage a more solid contact.

Ball position: Towards the front half of the stance - This enables the club to follow the slope and work with it rather than against it. It also allows the shoulders and body to position itself parallel with the slope.

Stance/posture: The body (shoulders and hips) are to be positioned parallel with the slope; in essence the body is following the contour of the slope. This automatically places more weight on the back foot.

Swing: The follow through may be a little shortened depending on the severity of the slope. The priority here is to maintain balance throughout. As with any sloping lie it is worth sacrificing a little distance in favour of maintaining balance and quality of contact. There may be a necessity to 1 or 2 extra clubs to counteract the extra height gained due to the slope.

Downhill Lie

Ball Flight Tendency: Will travel right in the air & lower trajectory

The slope will take loft away from the golf club hence creating a lower ball flight. As the body marries up with the slope during the set up it also causes the body motion and weight distribution to become more restricted. The angle of attack into the ball steepens and as the club follows the slope through impact, hand and clubface rotation becomes more limited, it will feel as though the clubface is being 'held off', encouraging the ball to travel to the right.

Aim: Aim the leading edge of the club face to the left of target, the amount dependant on the severity of the slope. The feet, hips and shoulders will be parallel to this target line.

Grip: As normal. If the slope is particularly severe, grip down slightly to avoid the slope getting in the way during the downswing and to encourage a more solid contact.

Ball Position: Position the ball towards the back half of the stance. This enables a solid contact and avoids hitting the ground before the ball.

Stance/posture: Position the shoulders and hips parallel to the slope, the body and club want to follow the slope at all times. The weight will now favour the front foot.

Printed in Great Britain
by Amazon